STARS AROUND MY SCARS

STARS AROUND MY SCARS

The Annotated Poetry *of* Taylor Swift

Dr. Elly McCausland
Professor of Swifterature

Andrews McMeel Publishing
a division of Andrews McMeel Universal
1130 Walnut Street, Kansas City, Missouri 64106

www.andrewsmcmeel.com

Edited by Monica Sweeney
Design by Melissa Gerber
Cover image copyright BigArtLab via Creative Market

Images used under license by Shutterstock.com

25 26 27 28 29 LAK 10 9 8 7 6 5 4 3 2 1

ISBN: 979-8-8816-0081-5

Library of Congress Control Number: 2024948577

For Mary Brown and Doreen McCausland,

always still all around.

I wish I'd asked you to write it down for me.

Contents

introduction

"Is Taylor Swift a poet?"

It's a question I've received countless times since establishing my Masters course, "English Literature (Taylor's Version)," at Ghent University in 2023, and even more so since Swift released her eleventh studio album, *The Tortured Poets Department*, in 2024. We've been spotting literary references in Swift's work for years, ever since she name-checked *Romeo and Juliet* in "Love Story" in 2008. Yet something about her claiming the title "Chairman of the Tortured Poets Department" and releasing an album titled *The Anthology*, containing tracks like "The Manuscript," prompted a new line of questioning that was often accompanied by a slight air of disbelief. Is it even possible, people asked me, that this global superstar, best known for her breakup anthems, could call herself *a poet?*

The idea that it would be radical to consider Swift a poet needs some unpacking, not least because of what it tells us about an apparent mismatch in the public imagination between "high" culture and "popular" culture. To many, poetry is still considered an elite art form, more closely associated with ruff-wearing men from centuries ago than glitter-clad, high-heeled, blonde pop stars. Yet Swift herself has described her love of penning songs in what she calls the "quill" and "fountain pen" genres, drawing inspiration from figures like Charlotte Brontë and Emily Dickinson when doing so. Poetry is, in fact, one of the most ancient and diverse forms in literature, taking the shape of everything from epic to sonnet to haiku, limerick to ballad to ode, free verse to rhyming couplets. Scholars have been debating the question "what is a poem?" for centuries, with no concrete answers.

Enter Swift, whose lyrics make use of a wealth of literary features commonly found in texts widely considered to be poetry (you can find a full list of these in the **glossary**). Her writing is diverse, spanning a huge range of themes (unsurprising in a body of work that extends to nearly 300 songs) and playing with language in innovative ways, much like the best poets. If we consider the fact that some of the earliest poetry would have been set to music and performed, we might question whether there is really that much difference between the musical lays of the medieval French troubadours, which often dealt with unrequited love, and Swift, clad in a text-covered dress, proclaiming soulfully "I love you, it's ruining my life" on stage at the Eras Tour.

Swift is often dismissed as "only" writing about boys and breakups. In addition to the fact that this simply isn't true (the stats are widely cited online: less than a third of Swift's songs deal explicitly with a breakup), it also ignores her songwriting skill and craft. This book aims to showcase not just the diversity of Swift's broad oeuvre, but also her careful construction of every individual line. Swift is, first and foremost, a storyteller. Her songs have a remarkable ability to condense a sweeping, sometimes epic narrative into just a few lines, often taking the listener on a journey alongside the speaker through a wealth of emotions and reactions. Particularly notable is Swift's frequent use of images that have gone on to gain their own famous afterlives: a red scarf in a drawer, a spinning mirrorball, a cardigan under someone's bed. This technique has become tightly linked to the intricate lore of her work—what is sometimes only half-jokingly referred to as the "Taylor Swift cinematic universe"—but is also responsible for the relatability of Swift's lyrics and thus, in part, her enormous success. Those images prompt us to consider similar tableaux, flashbacks, and snapshots from our own lives, which have become saturated with meaning in our memories. The intense specificity of Swift's images therefore creates a paradox, as they make her music universally understandable.

Swift has been drawing "stars around our scars" (as she sings in "cardigan") for the best part of two decades. Now, with this book, I've tried to draw stars around her most important lyrics and get to the bottom of her eminently relatable, consolatory, and empowering writing.

Literary analysis of poetry is concerned with the relationship between form—the words on the page and where they are placed—and content or meaning: what the poem seems to be *about.* You'll see from reading this book that Swift's use of rhyme, figurative language, and imagery are tightly connected to the mood or feeling of each song, in ways you may never have considered before. I'll demonstrate how Swift really does have a way with words, often using language to surprise and prompt us to reconsider the metaphors, images, and clichés we use every day—again, much like the best poets. I'll show how she uses rhetorical techniques that date back to classical antiquity to reinforce her message. She may not put narcotics into all of her songs, but she does use tried-and-tested techniques to keep us singing along.

This book certainly doesn't claim to provide exhaustive explanations of all Swift's songs. I don't pretend to have noticed every single feature of

Swift's writing—I only point out examples of metaphor, imagery, alliteration, etc., when I have something to say about them—nor do I pretend that my interpretations are any more valid than yours. What I have tried to do, however, is to show how Swift uses poetic techniques in order to emphasize or support particular ideas, and how unpacking her poems more deeply in this way might enhance our analysis or understanding. I am not interested in conducting the "paternity tests" of her work that Swift so derided in the prologue to *Reputation*: you won't find rampant speculation here about which man or relationship each song is about. Rather, I explore the emotions, themes, and ideas behind each song, and how the language brings these to life.

In selecting the songs, I've tried to consider three criteria. First, songs that really highlight Swift's way with words: those that make use of clever rhetorical features to emphasize their main themes. Unsurprisingly, many of these are concentrated on the albums *folklore, evermore,* and *The Tortured Poets Department;* but you will also see Swift using such techniques as far back as her debut album. Second, fan favorites: songs that seem to resonate particularly strongly with listeners and have gained vivid afterlives in their own right, such as "All Too Well" and "You're On Your Own, Kid." Finally, songs that prove Swift is far more than just a writer of banging breakup anthems: those that reflect on growing up ("The Best Day"), the pressures of fame ("Nothing New"), and politics ("Miss Americana & The Heartbreak Prince"). I hope you find your favorites here, but if you don't, perhaps the techniques discussed in this book will help you to conduct your own analysis.

Next chapter.

a note on the text

Throughout this book, I distinguish between Swift herself and the person uttering the words of the song, whom I call "the speaker." In literary study, we separate the author of a poem and the persona who speaks or narrates the poem, recognizing that they are not the same: not all poetry is autobiographical, and even if it is, there are nearly always elements of fiction or embellishment, too. Although Swift identifies much of her work as autobiographical, she has also explicitly said—of albums such as *folklore* and *evermore*, for example—that she sometimes tells other people's stories, including those of fictional characters. The speaker, therefore, is the character who is expressing particular thoughts or feelings in each individual song. Of course, this probably sometimes overlaps with Swift herself, but we can never know for sure. I do refer to the speaker as "she," partly for consistency and partly because the speaker often seems to be, at least partially, an avatar of Swift herself, though I recognize that we might read the speaker's gender as ambiguous in many songs. Similarly, I also refer to the "object" of the song: the person, people, or things whom the speaker seems to be addressing. Where Swift has been explicit about this, I mention it (she has stated, for example, that "marjorie" is about her grandmother). Otherwise, I make some suggestions based on the words we have. Where the song is a love song and its object is unclear, I use the pronoun "he" for consistency, but I'm aware that this is sometimes ambiguous.

the manuscripts

I'll share connections that can be drawn from Taylor's lyrics to literary works throughout the coming manuscript—from poetry and plays to mythology and novels. Here they are for your reading pleasure:

"Daddy" by Sylvia Plath

Great Expectations by Charles Dickens

The Great Gatsby by F. Scott Fitzgerald

Greek mythology, including the stories of Actaeon, Cassandra, Diana, and Sisyphus

Jane Eyre by Charlotte Brontë

A Little Princess by Frances Hodgson Burnett

The Lovely Bones by Alice Sebold

"Ode: Intimations of Immortality from Recollections of Early Childhood" by William Wordsworth

Rebecca by Daphne du Maurier

Romeo and Juliet by William Shakespeare

The Scarlet Letter by Nathaniel Hawthorne

The Signature of All Things by Elizabeth Gilbert

"Sleeping Beauty" by Charles Perrault (or "Briar Rose" by The Brothers Grimm)

A Streetcar Named Desire by Tennessee Williams

The Sun Also Rises by Ernest Hemingway

"The Swallow" by Charlotte Smith

A Tale of Two Cities by Charles Dickens

"To a Mouse" by Robert Burns

A Wrinkle in Time by Madeleine L'Engle

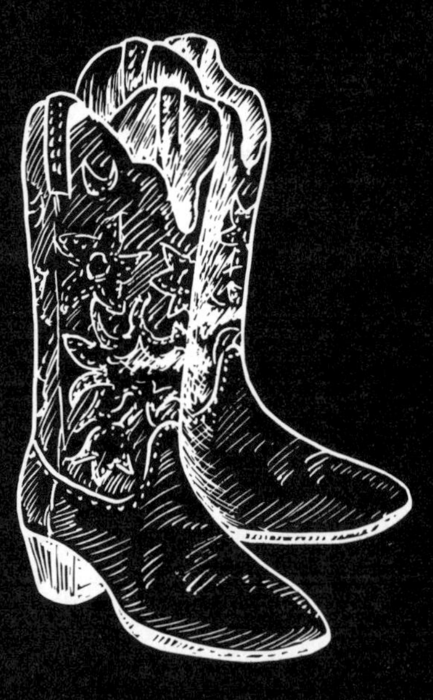

chapter one

TAYLOR SWIFT

Tim McGraw

The contrast between fantasy and reality are explored in more depth in Swift's later songs, like "White Horse"

He said the way my blue eyes shined
Put those Georgia stars to shame that night
I said, "That's a lie"
Just a boy in a Chevy truck
That had a tendency of gettin' stuck
On backroads at night

"he said" vs. "I said" = theme of miscommunication

Refusal to accept a clichéd compliment

ambiguous: the truck or his behavior?

And I was right there beside him all summer long
And then the time we woke up to find that summer gone

Rhyming couplet—time that seems to pass more quickly or slowly than it should is a Swiftian trope

But when you think Tim McGraw
I hope you think my favorite song
The one we danced to all night long
The moon like a spotlight on the lake
When you think happiness
I hope you think that little black dress
Think of my head on your chest
And my old faded blue jeans
When you think Tim McGraw
I hope you think of me

Situates Swift within the realms of country music, and foreshadows her tendency to name-check

Simile suggests the lake was a stage upon which they enacted their romance

An item of clothing is often highly symbolic

Anticipates "Wildest Dreams"

September saw a month of tears
And thankin' God that you weren't here
To see me like that
But in a box beneath my bed
Is a letter that you never read
From three summers back

A significant artifact loaded with meaning

The letter contains the sentiments voiced in the song

It's hard not to find it all a little bittersweet

A defining feature of Swift's songwriting

And lookin' back on all of that, it's nice to believe

Retrospection is central to Swift's lyrics

Implies that the speaker realizes she's only engaging in a fantasy; he doesn't actually think of her

chorus repeats

And I'm back for the first time since then

I'm standin' on your street

And there's a letter left on your doorstep

And the first thing that you'll read

Is, "When you think Tim McGraw

The events discussed in the song turn out to be the song itself. It shows a "meta" tendency, and the enjambment creates a pause before the big reveal

I hope you think my favorite song

Someday you'll turn your radio on

I hope it takes you back to that place"

When you think happiness

I hope you think that little black dress

Think of my head on your chest

And my old faded blue jeans

When you think Tim McGraw

I hope you think of me

Repetition suggests that deep down, she knows she cannot control the outcome

Oh, think of me, mmm

"Hope" has become an actual command—the speaker really wants to control the narrative

He said the way my blue eyes shined

Put those Georgia stars to shame that night

I said, "That's a lie"

TIM MCGRAW

[analysis]

In this, Swift's first single, we see a lot of clues that foreshadow the songwriter she would go on to become. First, the bittersweet sensations that accompany the reviewing of a past relationship. Second, the taking of clichéd phrases and twisting them to create new meaning. Third, the "meta" tendency to refer to the process of songwriting within the song itself, or to create layers of narration by singing about the song. The song jumps around in time, from a past memory to the present day, to a present hope that the future will include memory of the past. The symbolic artifact of the unsent letter bridges these three different time zones, as the famous scarf from "All Too Well" would go on to do many years later.

The ability of single images to conjure up a wealth of emotion, something that would become one of Swift's defining songwriting traits, is clear in this song: the little black dress, blue jeans, Georgia stars, and unsent love letter all serve as symbolic shorthand for bittersweet sensations. They arguably encourage the listener to reflect on his or her own relationship relics, and are thus an early example of the lyrical relatability that is at the heart of Swift's popularity and success today. Swift's naming of Tim McGraw is an homage to, and an acknowledgment of, the country tradition in which she is a new participant, but also reflects the struggle of an emerging artist to find "A Place in This World," as another track from her debut album reads. Swift is a highly intertextual writer, making frequent allusions to other artists, literature, and popular culture as a means of articulating and placing her own unique voice and style. The speaker's concern with how the object of the song thinks of her links to the theme of controlling one's narrative and reception, something that would become key to Swift's later writing.

Cold As You

The whole song is about how easy the object has it, compared to the speaker

You have a way of coming easily to me
And when you take, you take the very best of me
So I start a fight 'cause I need to feel somethin'
And you do what you want 'cause I'm not what you wanted

Repetition emphasizes the unequal power dynamic and a loss of self to such unequal pairings

Self-destructive and self-sabotaging tendencies; anticipates "The Way I Loved You"

Parallelism

Oh, what a shame
What a rainy ending given to a perfect day

Implies control on the part of the object and powerlessness of the speaker

Pathetic fallacy: the weather reflects the speaker's mood

Just walk away

Anticipates Swift's favorite metaphors: words as weapons

Ain't no use defending words that you will never say
And now that I'm sittin' here thinkin' it through

Epiphany

I've never been anywhere cold as you

Imperative—seems to be the speaker talking to herself, but perhaps advice to the listener

Double negative for emphasis

You put up the walls and paint them all a shade of gray
And I stood there loving you, and wished them all away
And you come away with a great little story
Of a mess of a dreamer with the nerve to adore you

Present participle suggests this love has been ongoing, which makes its lack of reciprocity even sadder

Dialogismus

Disillusionment and broken dreams form a key part of her music

Sarcasm—the speaker is imagining how the object of the song might mock her devotion

Oh, what a shame
What a rainy ending given to a perfect day
So just walk away
Ain't no use defending words that you will never say
And now that I'm sittin' here thinkin' it through
I've never been anywhere cold as you

You never did give a damn thing, honey
But I cried, cried for you

Term of endearment contrasts jarringly with "damn"

Anticipates "you kept me like a secret" from "All Too Well." Double negative is emphatic

And I know you wouldn't have told nobody if I died, died for you

Died for you

Internal rhyme of "cried" and "died," along with hyperbole, contrast with the object of the song, who gives nothing

Oh, what a shame

What a rainy ending given to a perfect day

Oh, every smile you fake is so condescending

Countin' all the scars you've made

Now that I'm sittin' here thinkin' it through

I've never been anywhere cold as you

Subtle addition to the chorus highlights despair to righteous anger and realization, highlighting Swift's notable tendency to take her listener on a journey with all her songs. Music journalist Nate Sloan terms this the "time shift"

Counting as if they are trophies is somewhat sinister and bolsters the object's image as sadistic and uncaring

This song utilizes language that seems to indicate the speaker talking to herself, but again might be her message to the listener. This establishes something key to Swift's success: the feeling that you are listening to a friend who has experienced the same things as you, and who can offer guidance in tough times

COLD AS YOU

[analysis]

“Cold As You” established Swift’s tendency of reserving track 5 on her albums for her most “emotionally vulnerable” songs. She has described the lyrics as some of the “best ever written” with her collaborator Liz Rose. The song details the realization that certain loves will always be unrequited, and that certain people will never change and do not necessarily deserve the time, energy, and feelings you give them.

Swift uses a number of literary techniques that she will hone and develop in her later writing, such as pathetic fallacy, parallelism, repetition, metaphor, and exclamation (apostrophe, or addressing the person or thing that cannot respond). The main conceit of the song is the idea of the (unrequited) lover as a place, a form of antiprosopopoeia that both emphasizes his inhuman(e) coldness (Swift is using pathetic fallacy, too) but also suggests his importance to her; he is an expansive space whom she inhabits and cannot escape. Swift herself referred to the notion of being “cold as you” as a “burn”—which in itself is a metaphor.

The “you” of the song shifts between referring to the

object (the undeserving lover) and seemingly to the speaker herself and/or the audience. We get the sense that the speaker is advising the listener not to waste time on those who are undeserving. The song progresses from passive, sad despair to righteous anger and realization with the subtle addition to the final chorus, establishing Swift's tendency toward what music journalist Nate Sloan terms the "time shift"—telling a whole story in a short song by making small changes to each repetition of the chorus. The use of "damn" in the penultimate verse emphasizes the speaker gaining clarity and ending the song with an indignant epiphany. Thus, with this song, Swift establishes the tone that has made her so popular, particularly with a female audience: sympathetic, empathetic, and providing gentle guidance drawn from her own experience. Through subtle lyrical shifts that parallel her evolving emotions, she concludes the song by pivoting away from the emotional space in which she began—this would go on to become something of a "signature move" for her.

Our Song

As with "Tim McGraw," this early song from Swift's oeuvre is full of examples of lyrical techniques she would hone and perfect in her later work. Most important is the layered narration: a song within a song, which also talks about a note on which is written the song. The end rhyme and internal rhyme throughout give the song a very structured, rhythmic, upbeat feel.

I was ridin' shotgun with my hair undone

In the front seat of his car

He's got a one-hand feel on the steering wheel

The other on my heart — *Zeugma*

I look around, turn the radio down

He says, "Baby, is something wrong?"

I say, "Nothing, I was just thinkin' how we don't have a song"

And he says

Swift excels at telling long stories in microcosm in the space of just one song

Our song is the slamming screen door

Sneakin' out late, tapping on your window

Softness of the "s" sounds here (sibilance) contrasts with the door slam

When we're on the phone, and you talk real slow

Sung slowly, the lyrics and music match perfectly

'Cause it's late, and your mama don't know

Our song is the way you laugh

The first date, "Man, I didn't kiss her, and I should have"

And when I got home, 'fore I said, "Amen"

The combination of tenses—beginning with the past and switching quickly to the present, and then back again, with repeated present participles in the chorus—adds to this sense of something circular or repeated; the car incident happened once, but the love we hear about in "Our Song" is ongoing.

Asking God if he could play it again

Repetition of present participle suggests something habitual, echoing the comfort of their relationship

I was walkin' up the front porch steps after everything that day

Had gone all wrong and been trampled on

And lost and thrown away

Got to the hallway, well on my way to my lovin' bed

I almost didn't notice all the roses

And the note that said

Complex layering: Swift experiments with stories-within-stories and the meta such as in "The Story of Us" and "The Manuscript"

Our song is the slamming screen door

Sneakin' out late, tapping on your window

When we're on the phone, and you talk real slow

'Cause it's late, and your mama don't know

Our song is the way you laugh

The first date, "Man, I didn't kiss her and I should have"

And when I got home, 'fore I said, "Amen"

Asking God if he could play it again

I've heard every album, listened to the radio

Hyperbole for emphasis

Waited for something to come along

That was as good as our song

There's also a message here about originality: unable to find the perfect song on other albums or the radio in order to express their feelings, the couple write their own. This is, of course, what Swift has been doing for her entire career: translating her emotions and life experience into music that will become "our song" or "my song" for her listeners. When she released *Speak Now (Taylor's Version)*, she declared the music to be "ours": hers and her fans'.

'Cause our song is the slamming screen door

Sneakin' out late, tapping on his window

When we're on the phone, and he talks real slow

'Cause it's late, and his mama don't know

Our song is the way he laughs

The first date, "Man, I didn't kiss him, and I should have"

And when I got home, 'fore I said, "Amen"

Askin' God if he could play it again, play it again

Oh, yeah

Oh, oh yeah

The frequent, regular rhyme—both end rhymes and internal rhymes—gives the song a structured, organized feel that fits with Swift's early music and the upbeat tempo and theme of this particular tune.

I was ridin' shotgun with my hair undone

In the front seat of his car

I grabbed a pen and an old napkin

And I wrote down our song

A classic volta, a twist at the end of the song (the song we are listening to about their song *is* their song). Surprising the listener is very common in Swift's work: she frequently twists clichéd words and phrases to make us think about language in new ways

chapter two

FEARLESS *(Taylor's Version)*

Love Story

This song is one of Swift's first to explicitly reference a literary text—two, in fact. It alludes to William Shakespeare's play *Romeo and Juliet* and Nathaniel Hawthorne's novel *The Scarlet Letter*.

We were both young when I first saw you

A recollection of a past relationship. The reference to youth also suggests innocence and naivety

I close my eyes and the flashback starts

I'm standing there

Analepsis. This whole song is, in fact, a flashback

On a balcony in summer air

Alludes to the famous "balcony scene" in Shakespeare's Romeo and Juliet. Swift uses a popular interpretation, despite there being no mention of a balcony in the play

See the lights, see the party, the ball gowns

Imperative that draws us more deeply into the story

See you make your way through the crowd

And say, "Hello"

Little did I know

Enjambment keeps the listener in suspense, just as the speaker was

That you were Romeo, you were throwing pebbles

Imagery is echoed across Fearless

Swift takes great liberties with these texts: *Romeo and Juliet* is, of course, a love story, but it's certainly not a happy one (it ends in a double suicide), nor are the protagonists a prince or princess. That is perhaps the point: the speaker has created her own fantasy based on a patchwork of tropes drawn from film and literature (mirrored in the confusingly ahistorical costumery and setting of the song's video), a fantasy that the speaker desperately wants the object of the song to simply slot himself into ("baby just say yes").

And my daddy said, "Stay away from Juliet"

A reference to the ongoing feud between the Montagues and the Capulets in Shakespeare's play

And I was crying on the staircase

Begging you, "Please don't go," and I said

Pause as if the speaker is hesitating before delivering her impassioned speech

Romeo, take me somewhere we can be alone

I'll be waiting, all there's left to do is run

You'll be the prince and I'll be the princess

Fairy-tale or medieval romance—this song is a patchwork of different literary and historical references

It's a love story, baby, just say, "Yes"

This line suggests that the speaker has the template for the love story all planned out

So I sneak out to the garden to see you

A literary trope that dates back to classical antiquity: the *locus amoenus*, or "pleasant place," a traditional secluded setting for romantic encounters

We keep quiet 'cause we're dead if they knew

Reads as drama or hyperbole from the perspective of a teenage girl, yet dark when we consider the tragedy of *Romeo and Juliet*

So close your eyes

Escape this town for a little while, oh, oh

'Cause you were Romeo, I was a scarlet letter

A somewhat strained allusion to Nathaniel Hawthorne's *The Scarlet Letter*

And my daddy said, "Stay away from Juliet"

But you were everything to me

I was begging you, "Please don't go," and I said

It is perhaps a comment on the ways in which our expectations of romance are drawn from popular culture, and we fall into the trap of expecting real life to match up neatly with these fantasies—particularly when we are young. The framing of the whole song with a comment about youth, and the final line which suggests it is *because* of youth, suggest that the entire fantasy was a product of adolescent dreaming.

Romeo, take me somewhere we can be alone

I'll be waiting, all there's left to do is run

You'll be the prince and I'll be the princess

It's a love story, baby, just say, "Yes"

Romeo, save me, they're trying to tell me how to feel

This love is difficult, but it's real *Somewhat ironic, since the speaker has framed the love with two works of fiction*

Don't be afraid. we'll make it out of this mess

It's a love story, baby, just say, "Yes" *Shift in power dynamic: at times, the speaker is begging Romeo and fashions herself at his mercy; at other times, she is giving him orders*

Read this way, "Love Story" in fact appears as the naive prequel to "White Horse" (and indeed Swift did comment that they were both inspired by the same man): its young speaker innocently fails to distinguish between fantasy and reality, setting herself up for disappointment and disillusionment when her lover turns out not to be Romeo, or a prince, after all.

And I got tired of **w**aiting

Wondering if you were ever coming around

My **f**aith in you was **f**ading *Pairs of alliteration emphasize her dwindling belief in him*

When I met you on the outskirts of town

And I said, "Romeo, save me, I've been feeling so alone

I keep waiting for you, but you never come *Another meta-literary comment on the fact that reality will never match up to the fantasy*

Is this in my head? I don't know what to think"

Potentially the key to the whole song

He knelt to the ground and pulled out a ring, and said

Line continues beyond the end rhyme

"Marry me, Juliet, you'll never have to be alone

I love you and that's all I really know

I talked to your dad, go pick out a white dress

A supposedly insurmountable problem is resolved almost ridiculously easily, emphasizing the naivety and fantasy

It's a love story, baby, just say, 'Yes'"

'Cause we were both young when I first saw you

Implies causation: this fantasy existed because of the speaker's youthful daydreams

"Love Story" might then be read in meta-literary terms, commenting upon our need to "escape this town"—the mundanity of our everyday—by indulging in fantasies that lend a glamorous, dramatic gloss to the quotidian. Just be careful not to let the fantasy go too far, or you'll end up disappointed.

The Best Day

I'm five years old

Present-tense opening transports us back in time to the speaker's memory

It's getting cold

I've got my big coat on

Language is subtly childlike, adding to the sense that we are hearing the young version of the speaker

I hear your laugh

And look up smiling at you

I run and run

Repetition adds to the feeling of freedom

Past the **p**umpkin **p**atch

Idyllic childhood fun

And the tractor rides

Look now, the sky is gold

The color associated with this album

I hug your legs

A simple but powerful image

And fall asleep on the way home

I don't know why all the trees change in the fall

Naivety of this makes it clear that it's a child speaking

But I know you're not scared of anything at all

Don't know if Snow White's house is near or far away

Idealized fairy tales versus reality is prominent on Fearless: see also "White Horse"

But I know I had the best day with you today

Opposition between "don't know" and "I know" demonstrates the speaker's mother as stability in an otherwise turbulent world

I'm thirteen now

And don't know how

My friends could be so mean

Youthful language we would associate with this age, which will resurface in "Mean" on Speak Now

I come home crying

And you hold me tight

And grab the keys

Mirrors "run and run," suggesting the speaker's upbringing was marked by freedom and adventure

And we drive and drive

Until we found a town far enough away

And we talk and window shop

'Till I've forgotten all their names

I don't know who I'm gonna talk to now at school

But I know I'm laughing *Juxtaposes the uncertainty of the future with the happiness of the present. The present will provide resilience*

On the car ride home with you

Don't know how long it's gonna take to feel okay

But I know I had the best day with you today

I have an excellent father

His strength is making me stronger *Polyptoton, for emphasis on the shared strength of both*

God smiles on my little brother

Inside and out he's better than I am

I grew up in a pretty house

And I had space to run and I *Literal and emotional*

had the best days with you *Subtle shift to plural—the speaker's childhood was composed of many of these "best days"*

There is a video I found

From back when I was three *Ekphrasis takes us on a journey to a "story within a story"*

You set up a paint set in the kitchen

And you're talking to me *Immerses the listener as if we too are watching the video*

It's the age of **p**rincesses and **p**irate ships

And the seven dwarfs *When read in hindsight of the imagery across her career: Swift has arguably never left this age*

And Daddy's smart

And you're the prettiest lady in the whole wide world

And now I know why the all the trees change in the fall *A credit to her formative years*

I know you were on my side

Even when I was wrong

And I love you for giving me your eyes

Staying back and watching me shine and *Imagery fits with gold sky*

I didn't know if you knew

So I'm taking this chance to say *Using a song to articulate important feelings is a common trope in Swift's work*

That I had the best day with you today *Continuity—every day with her mother has been the best*

THE BEST DAY

[analysis]

This song—a good example to show to people who argue that Taylor Swift "only writes breakup songs"—is addressed to the speaker's mother. It muses on the speaker's idyllic childhood, depicting it as a time of safety, security, and stability that enabled the speaker to grow older and wiser; she references this again on "Christmas Tree Farm." The present tense and frequent childlike phrases take the listener on an immersive journey back to that childhood, which was characterized both by glorious freedom but also the inevitable pains of adolescence; Swift revisits these in "Fifteen," on the same album.

As in several other Swift songs, we also have a frame narrative—a story within a story—as the speaker recalls a videotape of her three-year-old self, using the literary device of ekphrasis. The song juxtaposes childhood naivety and innocence with the wisdom that comes of growing older, articulated through the simple image of trees changing in autumn. It implies that the strength given to her by her childhood will enable the speaker to handle the challenges of the future. Swift has jokingly referred to herself as a "small family business," referencing the role her parents and brother have played in her career.

The repetition of "the best day," and the final line of the song, make it clear that the speaker is referring to *every* day spent with her mother. Using a song to articulate feelings that the speaker needs others to hear will surface later in Swift's music, for example in "this is me trying" and "mirrorball."

chapter three

SPEAK NOW *(Taylor's Version)*

Dear John

Anastrophe

Long were the nights when

My days once revolved around you

Metaphor implies that she is the Earth who orbits his sun = power imbalance

Enjambment

Counting my footsteps

Praying the **f**loor won't **f**all through again

Caesura (pause) before "again"; the speaker has been in this state of precarity before

And **m**y **m**other accused me of losing my **m**ind

But I swore I was fine

Assonance links "accused" and "losing"

You paint me a blue sky

And go back and turn it to rain

And I lived in your chess game

Pathetic fallacy: world around her ("blue sky," "rain") dependent upon how John treats her

But you changed the rules every day

Wondering which version of you I might get on the phone tonight

Well, I stopped picking up and this song is to let you know why

Musical equivalent of "breaking the fourth wall"

Play on words. A "Dear John" letter was a breakup letter during the Second World War

Dear John, I see it all now that you're gone

Wisdom of hindsight

Don't you think I was too young to be messed with?

Anthypophora: answering one's own question, and also a reprimand of his behavior

The girl in the dress, cried the whole way home

I should've known

Internal rhyme is poignant. A girl in her best dress during a first great romantic disappointment

Well, maybe it's me

And my **bl**ind optimism to **bl**ame

Or maybe it's you and your sick need

To give love then take it away

And you'll add my name to your long list of traitors

A strong word with serious connotations, suggesting a deluded narrative that "John" uses to justify his treatment of the speaker

Who don't understand

And I'll look back and regret how I ignored when they said

"Run as fast as you can"

Dear John, I see it all now that you're gone

Don't you think I was too young to be messed with?

The girl in the dress, cried the whole way home

Dear John, I see it all now, it was wrong

Don't you think nineteen's too young

The chess game of the first verse has now progressed into something darker

To be played by your dark, twisted games when I loved you so?

I should've known

Passive voice emphasizes the way the object of the song exploited the speaker's naivety

You are an expert at sorry and keeping the lines blurry

Internal half rhyme nicely mirrors the idea of blurriness in the relationship

Never impressed by me acing your tests

All the girls that you've run dry have tired lifeless eyes

'Cause you burned them out

Ambiguous: referring to the girls or their eyes. If the latter, it's a rather gruesome image

But I took your matches before fire could catch me

Passive construction aligns with victimhood

So don't look now

I'm shining like fireworks over your sad empty town

Antiprosopopoeia: John as a place rather than a person

Oh, oh

The simile here is triumphant, but also aligns her with an explosive force as if to remind him of her power

Dear John, I see it all now that you're gone

Don't you think I was too young to be messed with?

The girl in the dress, cried the whole way home

I see it all now that you're gone

Don't you think I was too young to be messed with?

The girl in the dress wrote you a song

Meta. Explicitly confirms that the "girl in the dress" is indeed her

You should've known

You should've known

Don't you think I was too young?

You should've known

This could refer to John, as it seems, or herself

DEAR JOHN

[analysis]

The title of this song probably has a double meaning, evoking the genre of the "Dear John" breakup letter while possibly alluding to the real-life object of the song. It occupies the significant "track 5" slot of *Speak Now*. "Dear John" contrasts the wisdom of hindsight with the naivety of youthful love, progressing from wistful recollection to angry accusation, as is common in many of Swift's songs that reflect on past relationships. It uses the conditional tense to explore the idea of regret, which Swift would develop in more detail in the song "Would've, Could've, Should've" on *Midnights*. The latter song's reference to being nineteen suggests that the two have the same object.

The shift from "you should've known" to "I should've known" and back again implies the speaker's reflective journey through self-blame (of her "blind optimism") to the eventual realization that she was a vulnerable victim in this affair: the frequent use of the passive voice points to her exploitation by the older "John." The speaker answers the question, "Don't you think I was too young?" herself, from a place of more knowledgeable hindsight. Having painted an image of her youthful innocence, she invites our sympathy; we can *only* see John as taking advantage.

We witness many Swiftian tropes in "Dear John," including love as a (ruthless) game—a concept that returns in "State of Grace" on *Red*—and the ability of love to color (or remove color from) one's world. The latter trope is particularly significant: the song begins with images of rainy skies, progresses to dark games and lifeless eyes, but climaxes with the imagery of shining fireworks, amplifying the speaker's epiphany through hindsight, and highlighting empowered realization of her innocence in an exploitative affair.

The Story of Us

This song is one of the earliest examples of a key extended metaphor in Swift's work: that of a relationship as an ongoing story. It exemplifies Swift's self-reflexive tendency to write about writing, but also her concern with controlling a narrative.

I used to think one day we'd tell the story of us
How we met and the sparks flew instantly
And people would say, "They're the lucky ones"
I used to know my place was the spot next to you
Now I'm searchin' the room for an empty seat
'Cause lately I don't even know what page you're on

A relationship as text is a Swiftian trope, as in "Cornelia Street" with "we were a fresh page on the desk"

Echoes "Sparks Fly"

Dialogismus. Imagining what other people are saying

Potentially a pun

Notice also that the final line of this verse hangs awkwardly, which mirrors the speaker's feelings

While the speaker muses early in the song on the story that she (or they) will tell listeners about the relationship, she also suggests that it is entirely out of her control; that she is reading the book rather than writing it.

Oh, a simple complication
Miscommunications lead to fallout
So many things that I wish you knew
So many walls up, I can't break through

What begins as a simple rhyme continues with "lead to fallout," which does not rhyme. Effective way to show their breakdown in synchronicity

Now I'm standin' alone in a crowded room

Paradox, and yet loneliness can be exacerbated when one is surrounded by people

And we're not speakin'

And I'm dyin' to know, is it killin' you

A showcase of hyperbole and extremity

Like it's killin' me? Yeah

Possibly anthypophora: she knows it is killing him

I don't know what to say since the twist of fate

When it all broke down

And the story of us looks a lot like a tragedy now

The relationship has changed genres, showing its fragility as a story

In this case, the speaker is imagining how her readers would respond to their story ("they're the lucky ones") if it in fact fell into the fairy-tale genre she hoped for—but then quickly decides the genre is, in fact, tragedy.

Next chapter

Speeds up the narrative in a Swiftian way, which often takes us on an epic journey in microcosm in just a few lines

How'd we end up this way?

See me nervously pulling at my clothes and tryin' to look busy

Imperative draws attention to the tableaux of vulnerability and anxiety

And you're doin' your best to avoid me

I'm starting to think one day I'll tell the story of us

A throwback to the opening line, showing us a shift

How I was losin' my mind when I saw you here

But you held your pride like you should've held me

Antanaclasis, emphasizing the tragic fact that the object holds an intangible grudge rather than embracing the present reality

Oh, I'm scared to see the ending

Here, the unfolding story is subject to the winds of fate, despite the song itself demonstrating her attempt to exercise control

Why are we pretending this is nothin'?

I'd tell you I miss you, but I don't know how

Once again, what could have been a neat end rhyme continues, disrupting the neatness to expose the relationship breakdown

I've never heard silence quite this loud

Oxymoron emphasizes that an absence of words can be a devastating, heavy presence

There is a constant tension in Swift's work between exercising control over her story and publicly stating that she no longer cares; between acting like a "Mastermind" and urging us to "call it what we want." Her fear of taking control at this point in her career is exemplified here, in one of her earlier songs, by the line, "I'm scared to see the ending."

chorus repeats

This is looking like a contest

Of who can act like they care less

But I liked it better when you were on my side

The battle's in your hands now

But I would lay my armor down

If you said you'd rather love than fight

Poignantly reflects the earlier, "I wish you knew"

So many things that you wish I knew

But the story of us might be ending soon

The verb "ending" in its intransitive sense is significant—implies their ending will happen as if by fate. We don't know who will end it, if anyone

The speaker wavers between feeling in control—"the story of us might be ending soon"—and helplessly at the mercy of the "twist of fate." It raises the wider question of how much control one ever does have over one's own story, particularly when there are other "characters" involved.

chorus repeats

And we're not speakin'

And I'm dyin' to know, is it killin' you

Like it's killin' me? Yeah

I don't know what to say since the twist of fate

'Cause we're goin' down — *Alludes to a sinking ship, a metaphor Swift uses again in "So Long, London"*

And the story of us looks a lot like a tragedy now

The end — *Spoken, cathartically enabling closure*

There's a sense in the song that this story might just end spontaneously, soon, and it's unclear who is to blame. This perhaps reflects the ways in which some relationships just come to an end through communication breakdown, without a clear culprit. Swift explores the idea of a relationship "postmortem" later, in "How Did It End?"

As with "Our Song," there's a meta aspect here: the "story of us" that the speaker discusses in the song *is* the song; this is clear from the spoken "next chapter" and "the end." In essence, she is regaining some authorial control of a story gone off the rails by reading it aloud in her own voice. This is rather fitting, after all, for an album titled *Speak Now.*

Innocent

No real rhyme here, which reveals an uneasy, lost feeling on the part of the object

Direct address

I guess you really did it this time

Left yourself in your warpath

Lost your balance on a tightrope

Lost your mind tryin' to get it back

Precarity of fame—Kanye West received a lot of criticism following his interruption of Swift at the MTV Video Music Awards

Wasn't it easier in your lunchbox days?

Always a **b**igger **b**ed to crawl into

Wasn't it beautiful when you believed in everything

And everybody believed in you?

Antimetabole here helps to highlight the period of complete trust and faith

It's alright, just wait and see

Your string of lights is still bright to me

Oh, who you are is not where you've been

You're still an innocent

The speaker has a level of omniscience: she has answers and can offer them as comfort

Rhyme and assonance in the chorus contrast the lack of rhyme in the opening verse

You're still an innocent

"An" is subtle but significant. It implies all-encompassing innocence

Did some things you can't speak of

But at night you live it all again

You wouldn't be shattered on the floor now

If only you had seen what you know now then

Hindsight and regret surface frequently in Swift's work, for example in "Would've, Could've, Should've"

Wasn't it easier in your firefly-catchin' days?

And everything out of reach

Contrasts implicitly with the object's "string of lights" that have gone out

Someone **b**igger **b**rought down to you

Alliteration echoes "bigger bed" above

Wasn't it beautiful runnin' wild 'til you fell asleep

Anaphora—she understands

Before the monsters caught up to you?

Metaphor that fame spawns its own kind of monsters

It's alright, just wait and see

Your string of lights is still bright to me

Oh, who you are is not where you've been

You're still an innocent

It's okay, life is a tough crowd

Invokes celebrity, which fits with the intended object of the song

Thirty-two and still growin' up now

Who you are is not what you did

You're still an innocent

The core message of forgiveness, but the parallelism reminds us of our tendency to think people are what they do

Time **t**urns flames to embers

You'll have new Septembers

A metaphor suggesting the scandal will blow over. Once the fire is gone, the "string of lights" will burn more brightly

Everyone of us has messed up too, ooh, ooh

Minds change like the weather

A simile that indicates the fickle nature of public opinion

I hope you remember

Today is never **t**oo late to **b**e **b**rand new

Oh, oh, oh, oh, oh, oh

The alliteration highlights that it's always possible to make a change for the better

chorus repeats

It's okay, life is a tough crowd

Thirty-two and still growin' up now

Who you are is not what you did

You're still an innocent

You're still an innocent

Lost your balance on a tightrope, oh

It's never too late to get it back

The subtle shift from "lost your mind trying to get it back" in the opening verse sees the song conclude on a positive, soothing note

INNOCENT

[analysis]

"Innocent" seems to fit with Swift's more sentimental songs about childhood, such as "Never Grow Up" and "The Best Day," but it offers a surprise toward its end: it's actually about an adult. The thirty-two-year-old in question is Kanye West, to whom Swift publicly dedicated the song as a gesture of forgiveness after his notorious interruption of her acceptance speech at the 2009 MTV Video Music Awards. Swift has described the song as an expression of empathy, claiming that it taught her a lot about putting herself into someone else's shoes. We see this in the frequent rhetorical questions, which suggest that the speaker deeply understands the object of the song, and the difficulties he faces in the complicated world of fame and celebrity. The lack of rhyme in the verses is slightly awkward, and fits the description of things gone awry, but the chorus then uses frequent rhyme and assonance as if to suggest the speaker smoothing over the difficulties and offering the object of the song soothing consolation to make everything make sense once again.

The song uses spare but evocative images of childhood that highlight its joy, wildness, and simplicity. It suggests that the monsters we fear as children are actually far less frightening than the monsters we encounter as adults: gossip, judgment, and prejudice. There's a contrast between different images of light in the song: the string of lights versus the flames, emphasizing that the fire will die down and leave something pure and aglow, reminiscent of the fireflies the "innocent" used to catch. Note, too, the use of the phrase "*an* innocent," rather than just innocent: this suggests that innocence permeates the object's whole character, rather than being related to a particular deed or action. This helps to associate him with childhood naivety and wonder, offering Swift a tidy way to absolve the object of his messy and therefore very adult interjection into her narrative.

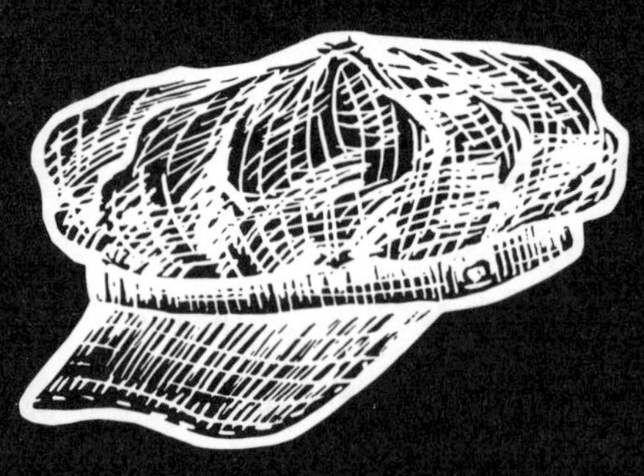

chapter four

RED *(Taylor's Version)*

Red

The song is full of similes as the speaker tries to find the right words to describe the love affair

Loving him is like driving a new Maserati down a dead-end street
Internal rhyme
Faster than the wind, passionate as sin, ending so suddenly
Loving him is like trying to change your mind
Internal (slant) rhyme
Once you're already flying through the free fall
Like the colors in autumn, so bright, just before they lose it all
Typically a color of sadness/depression
Losing him was blue, like I'd never known
Missing him was dark gray, all alone
Ambiguous: what is all alone?
Forgetting him was like trying to know
Somebody you never met
Paradox
But loving him was red
Loving him was red
Typically a color of passion, erotic love, and anger

Direct address to the listener implies they can relate

Ambiguous use of "it"—lose what? This line seems to be more about the love than about autumn leaves

The chorus switches between metaphor (was) and simile (was like)

Touching him was like realizing all you ever wanted
Was right there in front of you
Memorizing him was as easy as knowing all the words
To your old favorite song
Second person pronoun—makes it more relatable
Fighting with him was like trying to solve a crossword
And realizing there's no right answer
No rhyme-sounds slightly odd, doesn't fit—just like a crossword with no right answer
Regretting him was like wishing you never found out
That love could be that strong

Losing him was blue, like I'd never known
Missing him was dark gray, all alone
Suggests the absence of color—it has drained away with the loss of him
Forgetting him was like trying to know
Somebody you never met

But loving him was red

Oh, red

Burning red *Emphasizes red as associated with heat and passion also suggests a negative side—burning is, of course, painful*

Remembering him comes in flashbacks and echoes

An imperfect imprint; the memories are not entirely accurate or complete

Tell myself it's time now gotta let go

But moving on from him is impossible

When I still see it all in my head

In burning red

Burning, it was red

Oh, losing him was blue, like I'd never known

Missing him was dark gray, all alone

Forgetting him was like trying to know

Somebody you never met

'Cause loving him was red

Suggests all of the above (how difficult it is to forget) is specifically because the love was so painful

Yeah, yeah, red

Burning red

And that's why he's spinning 'round in my head

Comes back to me, burning red

Yeah, yeah

His love was like driving a new Maserati down a dead-end street

Song ends on the idea of a dead end, just like the relationship

RED

[analysis]

"Red" uses a list of similes and metaphors with varying degrees of logic as the speaker tries to find the right words and concepts to describe a tempestuous love affair. The core image, driving a fast car down a dead-end street, emphasizes it as a whirlwind romance that ended almost as soon as it started, but also hints at the emotional violence caused by its "car crash" ending. A sports car features prominently on the album cover for *Red (Taylor's Version),* serving perhaps as a central metaphor for this emotionally turbulent period of music, as Swift illustrates the formative period of her early twenties.

"Red" runs through colors associated with various stages of the affair: blue for sadness, gray for depression, and red to signify the vivid, all-consuming but hurtful nature of the love (orange is also implied in the reference to autumn colors). Similarly, the references to "burning" highlight the passion but also the pain. This is also hinted at in the phrase "passionate as sin." The negative connotations of "sin" allude to the relationship being problematic and doomed from the start. The song's use of the second person renders the lyrics more universal, encouraging the listener to relate to them personally and to identify with the speaker.

The rhyme is inconsistent—sometimes internal, sometimes absent, sometimes slant rhyme—which mirrors the inconsistency and turbulent nature of the affair itself. Notice the way the song begins with "loving him *is* like," and ends with "his love *was* like." The time shift here is a sad reminder that the love affair is now definitely over, yet the contrasting present tense in "he's spinning" and "comes back to me" suggest that the speaker is unable to forget. "Red" uses multiple contrasts and paradoxes to suggest the love was conflicted from the beginning: a metaphorical dead end, "like a crossword puzzle with no right answer."

All Too Well *(10 Minute Version)*

I walked through the door with you, the air was cold

In media res

But something 'bout it felt like home somehow

Adnomination

And I left my scarf there at your sister's house

A simple object becomes invested with a wealth of meaning because of the emotions surrounding it

And you've still got it in your drawer, even now

Apostrophe, used frequently in odes

Oh, your sweet disposition and my wide-eyed gaze

Synecdoche: he is represented by his disposition, and her by her gaze

We're singing in the car, getting lost upstate

Autumn leaves falling down like pieces into place

Beauty but also loss

The rhyme becomes more and more perfect as this verse moves on, as if the poetic pieces are falling into place too

And I can picture it after all these days

Slightly meta, since the song is the result of her memories

And I know it's long gone and

That **m**agic's not here no **m**ore

The polysyndeton and enjambment here add to the feeling that what we are hearing is unfiltered

And I might be okay, but I'm not fine at all

Very Swiftian use of two apparent synonyms that points out their differences

Oh, oh, oh

'Cause there we are again on that little town street

Memories of the past can sometimes haunt us, unbidden

You almost **r**an the **r**ed 'cause you were lookin' over at me

Wind in my hair, I was there

I remember it all too well

Not just "well," but "all too well": the clarity of the memories is painful

Photo album on the counter, your cheeks were turning red

Use of participle lends a sense of immediacy

Image plunges us into the scene

You used to be a little kid with glasses in a twin-sized bed

And your mother's telling stories 'bout you on the tee-ball team

You taught me 'bout your past, thinking your future was me

Almost filmic in transition

And you were tossing me the car keys, "fuck the patriarchy"

Key chain on the ground, we were always skipping town

Enjambment subtly exposes the object as potentially using feminist slogans to be "quirky," and therefore hints to the listener not to take him entirely seriously

The end rhyme and internal double rhyme create a sense of being in sync, a reflection of how the speaker feels

And I was thinking on the drive down, any time now

He's gonna say it's love, you never called it what it was

Sudden shift from past to present

'Til we were dead and gone and buried

Check the pulse and come back swearing it's the same

After three months in the grave

Polysyndeton amplifies the "gone-ness" of the relationship: not just gone or dead, but buried

And then you wondered where it went to as I reached for you

But all I felt was shame and you held my lifeless frame

The internal rhyme here draws more attention to the oppositions

And I know it's long gone and

There was nothing else I could do

And I forget about you long enough

To forget why I needed to

A relatable contradiction

'Cause there we are again in the middle of the night

We're dancing 'round the kitchen in the refrigerator light

One of Swift's very specific images that somehow paradoxically makes her lyrics more relatable

Down the stairs, I was there

I remember it all too well

And there we are again when nobody had to know

You kept me like a secret, but I kept you like an oath

An important opposition, suggesting the lover wanted to hide the relationship while she was nothing but devoted

Sacred prayer and we'd swear

Swift often frames love as religion, as in "False God" and "Guilty As Sin?"

To remember it all too well, yeah

Well, maybe we got lost in translation

Maybe I asked for too much

But maybe this thing was a masterpiece

'Til you tore it all up

Running scared, I was there

I remember it all too well

And you call me up again just to break me like a promise
So **c**asually **c**ruel in the name of being honest

This simile compares two things that are intangible and metaphorical: breaking a promise and breaking a person.

I'm a crumpled up piece of paper lying here
'Cause I remember it all, all, all

A very Swiftian metaphor to convey the depth of pain and rejection, but also the search for words to define oneself or relationship in full

They say all's well that ends well, but I'm in a new Hell
Every time you double-cross my mind

A twist on two common idioms: Her memories are intertwined with his betrayal

You said if we had been closer in age maybe it would have been fine
And that made me want to die

The song paints the lover as noncommittal throughout

The idea you had of me, who was she?

Anthypophora

A never-needy, ever-lovely jewel whose shine reflects on you
Not weeping in a party bathroom

Swift has invented compound adjectives, suggesting this ideal does not exist

Some actress asking me what happened, you
That's what happened, you
You who charmed my dad with self-effacing jokes
Sipping coffee like you're on a late-night show

A tableau to say without saying that the object is self-assured and charming but problematic underneath

But then he **w**atched me **w**atch the front door all night, **w**illing you to come
And he said, "It's supposed to be fun turning twenty-one"

This line is longer than the rest, as if to mirror how long she waited

Reworking a common phrase to express the loss in question

Time won't fly, it's like I'm paralyzed by it
I'd like to be my old self again, but I'm still trying to find it
After plaid shirt days and nights when you made me your own
Now you mail back my things and I walk home alone
But you keep my old scarf from that very first week
'Cause it reminds you of innocence and it smells like me
You can't get rid of it

A testatment to the ways in which relationships are often heavily tied with relics

'Cause you remember it all too well, yeah

'Cause there we are again when I loved you so — *Striking for its simplicity*

Back before you lost the one real thing you've ever known

It was rare, I was there

I remember it all too well

Wind in my hair, you were there

You remember it all

Down the stairs, you were there

You remember it all

It was rare, I was there

I remember it all too well

Potentially a pun, as the subsequent lines are full of blows and bruising

And I was never good at telling jokes, but the punch line goes

"I'll get older, but your lovers stay my age"

From when your **Br**ooklyn **br**oke my skin and bones

Suggests weight loss due to grief, but might also suggest that she has lost her "other half": him

I'm a soldier who's returning half her weight

And did the twin flame **b**ruise paint you **b**lue?

Just between us, did the love affair maim you, too?

Underscores the damage done

'Cause in this city's barren cold

The song returns full circle to its beginning, but this time the cold is not followed by a feeling of home

I still remember the **f**irst **f**all of snow

And how it glistened as it **f**ell

Pathetic fallacy: being with him made the snow beautiful

I remember it all too well

Just between us, did the love affair maim you all too well?

Just between us, do you remember it all too well?

extended chorus

ALL TOO WELL

(*10 Minute Version*)

[analysis]

Does this song even need an introduction? "All Too Well" is, for many, Swift's ultimate break-up anthem (and, of course, it's track 5 on *Red*.) She has said that it was initially far longer than the already-quite-long 5-minute track we got on *Red*, but fortunately her rerecording of *Red (Taylor's Version)* in 2021 enabled her to give us what we wanted: ten whole minutes of this epic narrative whose main characters are a red scarf and a refrigerator light. (And, probably, Jake Gyllenhaal, whose social media, and sister Maggie, were bombarded with questions about the whereabouts of the scarf in the wake of ATW10's rerelease).

I often use "All Too Well" as an example of what I call Swift's "universal specificity": her tendency to pepper her songs with hyper-specific images that paradoxically make them more relatable. They prompt the listener to recall similar moments, objects or sensations from their own lives, and remind us of the way love makes us invest even the most ordinary things with deeply personal meanings. The song is also an example of the way Swift takes us on an epic journey with her lyrics in just a few minutes, from the tender nascent beginnings of a relationship to its bitter legacy and lack of closure. She tends to swing back and forth between different emotions and modes (confessional, vengeful, elegiac) in the same song, mirroring the turbulence of our feelings in the wake of intense loss. "All Too Well" is rich in wordplay—including with its own title—as Swift toys with clichés to point out the inability of common platitudes to bring comfort or clarity in times of crisis: time *won't* fly; he's not *crossing* her mind but *double-crossing* it. The song rushes through similes and metaphors as if to express the inadequacy of language to capture deep emotional pain, searching for the right words like a writer constantly throwing out imperfect drafts—or crumpled up pieces of paper.

Nothing New (*From the Vault*)

Swift has spoken in interviews about the pressure an artist, and particularly a female artist, feels to constantly reinvent herself to maintain her success. This song muses on that pressure. It's perhaps significant that she duets with Phoebe Bridgers—another female artist, younger than Swift, who has been making music since high school—as if to emphasize the universality of this theme within the industry.

Unspecified "they," to represent a hostile (often partriarchal) public

They tell you while you're young
"Girls, go out and have your fun"
Then they hunt and slay the ones who actually do it
Criticize the way you fly when you're soaring through the sky
Shoot you down and then they sigh, and say
"She looks like she's been through it"

To emphasize the effect of misogynist hypocrisy

The use of sibilance evokes the whispering sound of the gossip

As in several other songs ("I Know Places," "the lakes"), Swift uses a general "they" to refer to the judgmental voices of the public, whom she frames as hunters and even killers. The sibilance of the first verse evokes the sound of constant gossip and whispers that, Swift suggests, are an inevitable part of female youth lived in the misogynist public eye. Yet she also seems to address that public intimately with the "you" of the song, fearing losing their attention. This captures the contradictory nature of fame: necessary dependence on a potentially hostile and fickle audience.

Lord, what will become of me
Once I've lost my novelty?

A prayer that is also a rhetorical question suggesting uncertainty and desperation

I've had too much to drink tonight
And I know it's sad, but this is what I think about
And I wake up in the middle of the night
It's like I can feel time moving

The passing of time as an almost physical sensation suggests the speaker's alertness and sensitivity to her own aging

How can a person know everything at eighteen but nothing at twenty-two?

The title of one of Swift's most famous songs, hinting at an anxiety that the speaker has peaked

Direct address to the listener

And will you still want me when I'm **n**othing **n**ew?

Implies that the speaker will have no value once she has lost her novelty

How long will it be cute

The behavior is only tolerated because of the speaker's charming naivety

All this crying in my room
When you can't blame it on my youth

Paradoxical view of youth in this song: alluring to an audience, but also easily dismissed

And roll your eyes with affection?

Suggests a patronizing attitude

"Nothing New" repeatedly contrasts youth and age, innocence and wisdom, and also suggests that female artists are viewed in starkly black-and-white terms: either as young, innocent and alluring (an "ingenue") or as past-it and unhinged ("breaking down"), with no gray area in between. If you're not new, you're nothing.

And my cheeks are growing tired

Synecdoche: her cheeks refer to her wider exhaustion

From turning red and faking smiles

Blushing with pleasure or shame

Ongoing pattern: the speaker must always put on charm

Are we only biding time 'til I lose your attention?
And someone else lights up the room?
People love an ingenue

Suggests an unhealthy public obsession with youth and innocence

I've had (I've had) too much to drink tonight

Slurred speech or voices inside the speaker's head

How did I go from growing up to breaking down?

The tragic pressure of "growing up precocious," as Swift terms it in "But Daddy I Love Him"

And I wake up (wake up) in the middle of the night

It's like I can feel time moving

How can a person know everything at eighteen but nothing at twenty-two?

Will you still want me when I'm nothing new?

I know someday I'm gonna meet her, it's a fever dream

Awareness of the unhealthiness of this obsession

The kind of radiance you only have at seventeen

Career as a literal path

She'll know the way, and then she'll say she got the map from me

I'll say I'm happy for her, then I'll cry myself to sleep

Anticipates the darker, weatherworn "but my bare hands paved their paths" from "Who's Afraid of Little Old Me?"

Oh, whoa, whoa

Oh, whoa, whoa, oh, whoa, oh

There are a number of allusions to Swift's other works, which seem to encourage us to interpret the song autobiographically. The song muses on the possibility that Swift has already peaked in her career—which, of course, turned out not to be true at all.

I've had (I've had) too much to drink tonight

But I wonder if they'll miss me once they drive me out

I wake up (wake up) in the middle of the night

And I can feel time moving

How can a person know everything at eighteen but nothing at twenty-two?

And will you still want me

Will you still want me

Will you still want me

The anaphora, or repetition of this phrase, suggests haunting anxiety

When I'm nothing new?

The anxieties expressed by Swift in this song are, themselves, nothing new. Writers have mused on the longevity of fame and speculated about their own legacies for centuries. Romantic poet William Wordsworth compared himself to the Carthaginian general Hannibal, seeing his poetic work as clearing a (metaphorical) path through the Alps for subsequent artistic generations. John Keats wrote miserably on his deathbed that he had "left no immortal work behind." Like Keats—whose work is often featured in poetry anthologies, taught in schools, and regarded as canonical English literature—Swift's worries seem to have been unfounded. There's something slightly surreal in hearing this vault track in hindsight, on the *Red* rerelease, when Swift's fame and success were still soaring to stratospheric heights.

chapter five

1989 *(Taylor's Version)*

Blank Space

Nice to meet you, where you been? *Confident nature of the speaker in this song: she's calling the shots*

I could show you incredible things *Conditional tense*

Magic, **m**adness, heaven, sin *Asyndeton—snapshots in quick succession—profile the instability of what's to come*

Saw you there and I thought

"Oh, my God, look at that face *Foreshadows drama*

You look like my next mistake

Love's a game, wanna play?" Ay *Swiftian metaphor*

New money, suit and tie *Summing him up in a phrase (synecdoche), emphasizes her ability to predict him based on his visible attributes*

I can read you like a magazine *Cheeky play on "read you like a book," but suggests a glossiness to him or a lack of depth*

Ain't it funny? Rumors fly

And I know you heard about me

So hey, let's be friends

I'm dying to see how this one ends *Speculating on the end of a relationship before it has begun, as in "Wildest Dreams"*

Grab your passport and my hand *Imperative reinforces the dominant role taken up by the speaker*

I can make the bad **g**uys **g**ood for a weekend

So it's gonna be **f**orever *Anaphora*

Or it's gonna go down in **f**lames

You can tell me when it's over, mm

If the high was worth the pain

Got a **l**ong **l**ist of ex-**l**overs

They'll tell you I'm insane *References to her own apparent insanity are frequent in Swift's oeuvre*

'Cause you know I love the players

And you love the game

'Cause we're young, and we're reckless
We'll take this way too far
It'll leave you breathless, mm
Or with a nasty scar
Got a long list of ex-lovers
They'll tell you I'm insane
But I've got a blank space, baby
And I'll write your name

Caesura

The metaphor works on many levels: a gap in dating or media headlines, a satirical notion that women are vacuous without men to lend meaning to their lives, or even a sexual euphemism. I like to think of it as Regency-era dance cards, where women would queue up their dancing partners for the night and carry around a list

Cherry lips, crystal skies
I could show you incredible things
Stolen kisses, pretty lies
You're the King, baby, I'm your Queen
Find out **w**hat you **w**ant
Be that girl for a month
Wait, the **w**orst is yet to come, oh, no
Screaming, crying, perfect storms
I can make all the tables turn
Rose garden filled with thorns
Keep you second guessing like
"Oh, my God, who is she?"
I get drunk on jealousy
But you'll come back each time you leave
'Cause, darling, I'm a nightmare **d**ressed like a **d**aydream

Both phrases highlight contradictions, juxtaposing something positive with something negative

Mocks the supposed drama of dating this speaker

Imperative hints at the chaotic nature of the verse to follow

A tricolon that also uses asyndeton to create a vivid montage for the listener

A fitting metaphor: something that is initially satisfying but ultimately poisonous

A warning of the pitfalls of judging by appearance alone. Which, ironically, is just what the speaker did in the first verse

extended chorus

BLANK SPACE

[analysis]

In this, one of Swift's best-loved and most well-known songs, she utilizes contrast and juxtaposition frequently to productive effect. Like another song on *1989*, "Wildest Dreams," "Blank Space" anticipates the end of a love affair before it has even begun. It positions the speaker and her prospective lover at a fork in the road, which will either lead to bliss or disaster. There are no gray areas in this song: it's magic or it's madness, it's heaven or it's sin. This is almost certainly intentional: Swift wrote the song as a deliberate riposte to those who criticized her dating life and framed her as the "crazy ex-girlfriend," a stereotype she leans into in the accompanying video in order to satirize it. The song is therefore full of hyperbolic language and juxtapositions, mocking the way in which patriarchal society so often views women in terms of extremes on a spectrum.

Despite the song's ostensible simplicity, it makes use of interesting literary devices such as synecdoche and asyndeton, and is rich in imagery. There is little complete rhyme, which lends the song a slightly conversational feel that fits with its opening and use of rhetorical questions and reported speech. The inconsistent rhyme also anticipates its themes of breakdown and fragmentation. As in many Swift songs, it relies on succinct, very visual tableaux to imply an emotional journey. These are offered almost as a list, often in incomplete sentences, which gives the impression of a whirlwind, dramatic affair. This is echoed in the song's video, which is also composed of dramatic montages: Swift smashing up a car with a golf club, stabbing a heart-shaped cake with a huge knife, and slashing a portrait on a wall (among others). There is also the recurring idea of love as a game, which is another very Swiftian trope—here, it's a game that is, paradoxically, both fun and miserable at the same time. The song's frequent use of repetition hints at the fact that the speaker will soon repeat all of these patterns again, with the next name on her list.

Clean

In media res

The drought was the very worst

(Oh-oh, oh-oh)

When the flowers that we'd grown together died of thirst

A metaphor suggesting a relationship that died due to a lack of nourishment and care

It was months and months of back and forth

(Oh-oh, oh-oh)

You're still all over me

Enjambment—one line "spilling" into the next—reflects the wine she is talking about

Like a wine-stained dress I can't wear anymore

Hung my **h**ead as I lost the war

And the sky turned black like a perfect storm

Rain came pouring down

When I was drowning, that's when I could finally breathe

And by morning

A pun that relies on a homophone—it could also be "mourning"

Gone was any trace of you, I think I am finally clean

Anastrophe

Extended metaphors of a relationship as a stain or dirt, and water to represent a period of grief and recovery

(Oh, oh, oh, oh)

There was nothing left to do

(Oh-oh, oh-oh)

When the butterflies turned to dust that covered my whole room

So I punched a hole in the roof

Allusion to "butterflies in the stomach," but the metaphor is made literal to highlight the residual traces of a love affair after it's dead

(Oh-oh, oh-oh)

Let the flood carry away all my pictures of you

The water filled my lungs, I screamed so loud

But no one heard a thing

Another paradox: she fights against the flood but later accepts it, finding life in "drowning"

Rain came pouring down

When I was drowning, that's when I could finally breathe

And by morning

Gone was any trace of you, I think I am finally clean

(Oh, oh, oh, oh)

I think I am finally clean

(Oh, oh) Oh, oh, oh, oh, oh-oh

Said, I think I am finally clean

(Oh, oh) Oh, oh, oh, oh, oh-oh

A central paradox runs through the song: drowning as breathing. Things had to get worse to get better. If the relationship was a drought, the flood perhaps represents the work the speaker has had to do to love herself afterward, and the process of recovery

Ten months sober, I must admit

Just because you're clean, don't mean you don't miss it

Ten months older, I won't give in

Now that I'm clean, I'm never gonna risk it

"Clean" previously referred to literal cleanliness, but now it's used in its idiomatic sense, to mean sober (from drugs or alcohol). She's clean in both senses—over the addiction and (almost) from the longing

chorus repeats

This connects with the sentiment in "loml": "I thought I was better safe than starry-eyed"

There are very few full rhymes in the song—rather, there are a lot of slant rhymes and assonance, which suggest the jarring, unnerving sense of grief experienced by the speaker, where nothing seems to make sense

CLEAN

[analysis]

The imagery of water is pervasive in this song, which puns on the idea of cleanliness as literal (free of dirt) and as metaphorical (sober, recovered from addiction). It explores the way in which a relationship can feel like it leaves physical traces, so marked that only a dramatic flood might wash them away—Swift also uses this idea in the song "You All Over Me." If drought expresses a relationship that "died" due to lack of nurture, the ensuing flood might be read as the speaker's investment in her own self, allowing the rain to pour down where before she had suppressed it. This explains why she can only breathe when drowning, or scream with lungs full of water—the flood might represent the work she has done to recover herself in the wake of an unfulfilling or neglectful relationship; only through this work can she breathe and thrive again. As in so many Swift songs, the central image works on multiple levels, and develops or shifts as the song progresses. The watery semantic field also anticipates "This Love," on the same album.

The lack of full rhymes, and frequent assonance, lend a sense of incompleteness, which intimates that the speaker is "clean" but still misses her lover. The imagery of cleanliness and breathing are common tropes in Swift's songs, which often frame intense emotion through its physical effects, and depict relationships leaving residual marks (most often, scars). The idea of being wary of taking a risk on a new love is also common in Swift's music, as is the (linked) metaphor of jumping into water as falling in love: see, for example, "Dancing With Our Hands Tied," "Paper Rings," and "Guilty As Sin?"

You Are In Love

Very little perfect rhyme in this song, making it feel conversational and spontaneous

One look, dark room

Meant just for you

Second person encourages the listener to insert themselves into this love story

Time moved too fast

You play it back

What the song is doing

Buttons on a coat

Lighthearted joke

No proof, not much

But you saw enough

This song is unusual in that the meter is comprised almost entirely of spondees, meaning that every syllable is equally weighted, which lends a sense of importance and depth to the very spare imagery

Small talk, he drives

Coffee at midnight

A simple image but one that reflects the way in which falling in love can be wildly disruptive and spontaneous

The light reflects

The chain on your neck

He says, "Look up."

Reported speech makes the listener feel as if they are there in the narrative

And your shoulders brush

No proof, one touch

But you felt enough

Repeated negatives in this verse contrast "enough"—we are attuned to the tiniest details when falling in love

You can hear it in the silence (silence), silence (silence) you

The chorus is full of paradoxes, as if to encompass the way in which falling in love defies logic and tangible evidence

You can feel it on the way home (way home), way home (way home) you

You can see it with the lights out (lights out), lights out (lights out)

You are in love, true love

You are in love

A progression from "dark room" to morning, then back to night again, reflecting the journey of the relationship

Morning, his place

Burnt toast, Sunday

You keep his shirt

He keeps his word

And for once you let go

Of your fears and your ghosts

One step, not much

But it said enough

You kiss on sidewalks

You fight then you talk

One night he wakes

Strange look on his face

Pauses, then says

"You're my best friend."

And you knew what it was

He is in love

chorus repeats

And so it goes

You two are dancing in a snow globe 'round and 'round

And he keeps a picture of you in his office downtown

And you understand now why they lost their minds and fought the wars

And why I've spent my whole life trying to put it into words

chorus repeats

Antanaclasis: "keep" is used in two different senses, literal and metaphorical, to prove or signal the characters' attachment

Hauntings of past loves are very Swiftian

Inanimate, intangible things being able to speak is key to this song

Perhaps a callback to "Sparks Fly"

Echoes the opening two lines; the story has come full circle

Caesura—the song pauses with the utterance it is describing

Love condensed in its own bubble, a kind of microcosm. The song is akin to the snow globe, encasing the lovers and immortalizing them

"They" seems to encompass all of humanity

A slightly jarring switch to "I" indicates that the song has been about the listener, and here Swift herself justifies her much-documented endeavor to write mostly love songs

YOU ARE IN LOVE

[analysis]

This song illustrates Swift's ability to tell an entire story in a series of well-chosen images. The unusual shortness of the lines in this song is particularly striking, encouraging the listener to connect them with a narrative of their own. The wealth of spondees lends gravitas to every image, reflecting the way in which simple moments or events take on a weighty significance where romantic love is concerned. It's almost as if we are listening to the speaker's stream of consciousness, as she flashes back to key moments of the relationship ("you play it back"), but they are phrased as if *we* are the ones experiencing them. In this way, the song seems to be universal, implying that we can all relate to these sensations. The paradoxes in the chorus play into the chaotic, often nonsensical feeling of true love, as does the relative lack of rhyme. Simultaneously, the repeated contrasts between "not much" and "enough" emphasize the subjectivity of love: a shoulder brush may not seem much but depending on the people and context it can contain a wealth of meaning, a language in itself that can be heard even in silence. The meanings we attach to small gestures and objects are a key focus in Swift's writing.

With the shift to "I" later in the song, we seem to hear Swift herself reminding us that the feeling of falling in love—which she has hitherto drawn us into, throughout the song—is so magical that she has been trying, her entire life, to find the right words to express it. It's perhaps a commentary on her much-discussed tendency to write love songs, and a justification: who *wouldn't* want to try and put this feeling into words? It's important to note the verb "trying," here, suggesting that she *still* hasn't found the right words. Many of Swift's later songs explore this idea, too.

Slut! (*From the Vault*)

This is the song that perhaps most effectively demonstrates Swift's technique of using a series of spare, succinct images loaded with meaning to conjure up a particular mood, period, or "era." It's almost as if we are watching a slideshow, with each moment flickering briefly before she moves on to the next. It begins with images of the vivid colors and textures of youth, perhaps recalling the line in "Out Of The Woods," from the same album: "we were in screaming color." There's a sense of naivety as the speaker is irresistibly drawn toward the mysterious "you" who is the song's object.

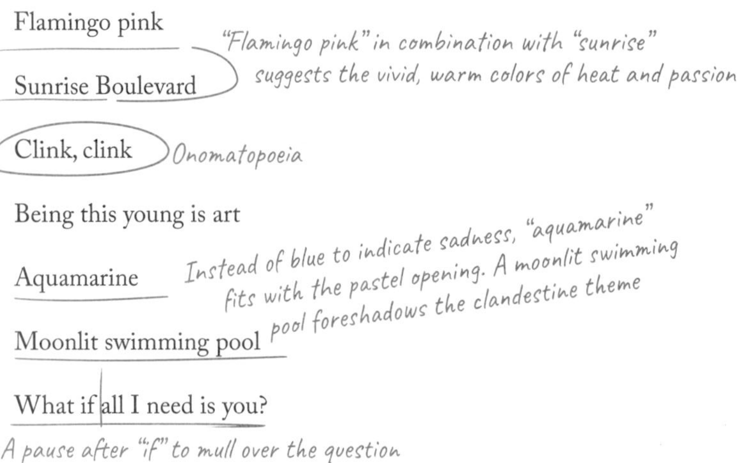

Flamingo pink
Sunrise Boulevard
"Flamingo pink" in combination with "sunrise" suggests the vivid, warm colors of heat and passion
Clink, clink
Onomatopoeia
Being this young is art
Aquamarine
Moonlit swimming pool
Instead of blue to indicate sadness, "aquamarine" fits with the pastel opening. A moonlit swimming pool foreshadows the clandestine theme
What if all I need is you?
A pause after "if" to mull over the question

The chorus uses adnomination, playing on multiple ideas related to the state of being in love, in order to explore the all-consuming nature of the romance the speaker discusses. Swift twists common phrases and idioms associated with falling in love, at times rendering them literal. The combination of love with sickness, drunkenness, smoke, and thorns implies the painful yet intoxicating side of this immersion in another person.

Got lovestruck, went straight to my head

A layered metaphor that combines a physical reading of "lovestruck" with the idea of love as intoxicating

Got lovesick, all over my bed

Anaphora. "Got" is in the passive voice—the speaker was powerless to resist

Adnomination

Love to think you'll never forget

A play on words that imagines "lovesick" as literal, but, because of the bed, hints at sexual interaction(s)

Handprints in wet cement

This love has clung to her

Adorned with smoke on my clothes

A word with connotations of finery: the speaker is proud to wear this love like a decoration

Lovelorn and nobody knows

Love thorns all over this rose

Hints that this love affair is not going to be untroubled

I'll **p**ay the **p**rice, you won't

Comment on misogynistic double standards

But if I'm all dressed up

They might as well be looking at us

And if they call me a slut

You know it might be worth it for once

Suggests the speaker has faced this judgment repeatedly

And if I'm gonna be drunk

Might as well be drunk in love

Send the code, he's waiting there

The **s**ticks and **s**tones they throw froze mid-air

Everyone wants him

That was my crime

The point here being that it is no crime at all

The wrong place at the right time

A twist emphasizing perhaps that the outcome is good for the speaker but not for those who accuse her of a "crime"

And I break down, then he's pullin' me in

In a world of boys, he's a gentleman

Got lovestruck, went straight to my head

Can also mean becoming arrogant; perhaps how the speaker imagines envious people talk about her

Got lovesick, all over my bed

Love to think you'll never forget

We'll pay the price, I guess

Shift to first-person plural—they're in this together

But if I'm all dressed up

They might as well be looking at us

If they call me a slut

You know it might be worth it for once

And if I'm gonna be drunk

I might as well be drunk in love

There is frequent end rhyme and assonance, all of which lend the song a neat, rhythmic feeling that mirrors the way in which the relationship inevitably unfolds. In fact, the song is concerned with that very inevitability, and the inescapable consequences of a love affair when one is in the public eye. Public scrutiny, and the experience of being "slut-shamed" as a woman in a patriarchal society riddled with sexist double standards, are common themes on *1989* in general, as Swift specifically mentions in the prologue to *1989 (Taylor's Version)* and later explores in "The Man" on 2019's *Lover*.

Half asleep

Taking your time

In the tangerine, neon light

Vivid colors return in this curious image. "Neon light" suggests the strip lighting of a public space, yet this is an intimate, private moment

This is luxury

Swift describes physical closeness as luxury in "King Of My Heart," but this implies the privacy itself is a luxury

You're not saying you're in love with me

But you're going to

Half awake

The same meaning as "half asleep," but suggests greater alertness and agency

Taking your chance

It's a big mistake

I said it might blow up in your pretty face

Potentially also an allusion to the consequences of public scrutiny

I'm not saying do it anyway

But you're going to

chorus repeats

This song explores the exquisite tension of questioning whether the risk of falling in love is worth it, while simultaneously succumbing to its inevitability.

chapter six

REPUTATION

...Ready For It?

The first song from Swift's *Reputation* sets up the style and tone of the coming album. It is concerned with knowledge, particularly of those we love: what we do and don't know about their past, how they help us to know ourselves better, what we think we know about our future together. The repeated question, "Are you ready for it?" is rhetorical: the speaker adopts a confident, determined tone that suggests she *knows* he is, in fact, ready. The intriguing ellipses (...) before the phrase in the title might stand for the "things" they do in the speaker's dreams: as if she has told him about them, before asking if he's ready.

Lack of "I" adds a spontaneous energy and emphasis on "knew," which is important in a song about what the speaker (thinks she) knows

Knew he was a killer first time that I saw him

Wondered how many girls he had **l**oved and **l**eft haunted

If he's the killer, then the girls would be haunting him. The power balance between the two figures shifts throughout the song

But if he's a ghost, then I can be a phantom

Pun

Holdin' him for ransom, some

Epizeuxis: use of "som"/"some" adds a staccato effect and a suspenseful pause

Some boys are tryin' too hard, he don't try at all though

First in a series of oppositions

Younger than my exes, but he act like such a man, so

I see nothing better, I keep him forever

Like a vendetta-ta

Simile that plays with the idea of keeping: in the physical sense of holding onto him, but also in the sense of retaining something in one's mind (the vendetta)

The song is also concerned with—of course—reputation: the personal and public baggage everyone brings to a new relationship, amplified tenfold in the case of a celebrity (as Swift will sing on the next track, "End Game": "ooh, you and me, we got big reputations"). The "he" shifts during the song to "you" and "we": within the microcosm of the song, we

get the whole story of attraction becoming romance. The object of the song has shifted from an abstract stranger with a reputation to someone the speaker knows intimately.

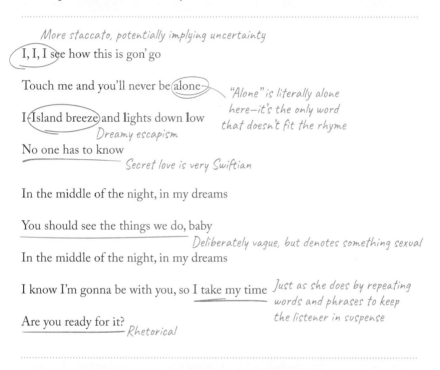

More staccato, potentially implying uncertainty

I, I, I see how this is gon' go

Touch me and you'll never be alone

"Alone" is literally alone here—it's the only word that doesn't fit the rhyme

I-Island breeze and lights down low

Dreamy escapism

No one has to know

Secret love is very Swiftian

In the middle of the night, in my dreams

You should see the things we do, baby

Deliberately vague, but denotes something sexual

In the middle of the night, in my dreams

I know I'm gonna be with you, so I take my time

Just as she does by repeating words and phrases to keep the listener in suspense

Are you ready for it?

Rhetorical

The language of robbery and murder run through the song, foreshadowing other tracks on the album—"Getaway Car" and "Look What You Made Me Do," for example— while also suggesting a power struggle reflected in the repeated reference to "games." The song makes frequent use of contrasts and oppositions—thief and jailer, killer and ghost, boy and man—which also reveal shifting power relations. The thief/jailer pairing in particular hints at the complexity of these power relations: the speaker adopts an omniscient, confident tone, but in likening her lover to her jailer also implies herself to be at his mercy (clear in later songs on the album).

Knew I was a robber first time that he saw me

This repeats the sentence structure of the first verse, but flips to his perspective

Stealing hearts and running off and never sayin' sorry

Polysyndeton + three present participles as if he literally caught her in the middle of these actions

But if I'm a thief, then he can join the heist, and

We'll move to an island, and

Words in the semantic field of crime fit the tone of Reputation, particularly "Getaway Car"

And he can be my jailer, Burton to this Taylor

Every love I've known in comparison is a failure

A pun and reference to famously troubled Hollywood couple Richard Burton and Elizabeth Taylor

Neatness in this double rhyme

I forget their names now, I'm so very tame now

The speaker as a caged animal occurs in songs like "I Know Places" and "Who's Afraid of Little Old Me?"

Never be the same now, now

Heightening the sense of repetition emphasizes how this love has affected her

I, I, I see how this is gon' go

The repetition of "I" sounds reaffirms how the speaker's confident certainty in her fantasies

Touch me and you'll never be alone

I-Island breeze and lights down low

No one has to know (No one has to know)

In the middle of the night, in my dreams

You should see the things we do, baby

In the middle of the night in my dreams

I know I'm gonna be with you, so I take my time

Are you ready for it?

Oh, are you ready for it?

The frequent repetition of certain words or syllables creates a kind of staccato effect that adds suspense, forcing us to wait for the next line: the speaker is *literally* "taking her time." There's a sense that we—the listener, and perhaps the object of the song, too—are being tested: are we ready for it?

Baby, let the games begin

Let the games begin

Let the games begin

Baby, let the games begin

Let the games begin

Let the games begin

This repeated imperative is slightly ambiguous: it sounds like she's addressing her lover, but the phrase itself denotes public entertainment. This fits with the theme of knowing versus not knowing in the song, and the general concern of Reputation with publicity and spectacle

chorus repeats

Getaway Car

No, nothin' good starts in a getaway car

Contrast amplified by alliteration—a getaway car signals the end of something

It was the best of times, the worst of crimes

Allusion to Charles Dickens's A Tale of Two Cities—but swaps "times" for "crimes" to signal the song's focus on (initially satisfying) wrongdoing

I struck a match and blew your mind

Reinterprets this phrase literally, connecting the destructive sparks the speaker kindled in her lover

But I didn't mean it, and you didn't see it

Slant rhyme hints that they are out of sync

The ties were black, the lies were white

Literal to metaphorical

In shades of gray in candlelight

I wanted to leave him, I needed a reason

Treasure map or "ex"

"X" marks the spot where we fell apart

He poisoned the well, I was lyin' to myself

Both parties are guilty of a "crime" of sorts: her lying to herself is similarly criminal

I knew it from the first Old Fashioned, we were cursed

We never had a shotgun shot in the dark (oh!)

Making the metaphor literal—the shot in the dark is now specifically a gunshot

You were drivin' the getaway car

We were flyin', but we'd never get far

Don't pretend it's such a mystery

Think about the place where you first met me

Imperatives—an order to her companion in the getaway car

Ridin' in a getaway car

There were sirens in the beat of your heart

A metaphor to suggest the love was doomed from the beginning

Should've known I'd be the first to leave

Think about the place where you first met me

In a getaway car, oh-oh-oh

No, they never get far, oh-oh-ah

No, nothin' good starts in a getaway car

Possible allusion to the 1963 film

It was the great escape, the prison break

Possible allusion to the TV series

The light of freedom on my face

Contrasts the gray and candlelight in the first verse

But you weren't thinkin' and I was just drinkin'

While he was runnin' after us, I was screamin', "Go, go, go!"

This is indeed shouted in the actual song

But with three of us, honey, it's a sideshow

And a circus ain't a love story, and now we're both sorry (we're both sorry)

A media circus, or possibly that the speaker was simply "performing" and didn't really feel it

Repeated as if to suggest the object's voice, too—they really are both sorry

chorus repeats

We were jet-set, Bonnie and Clyde (oh-oh)

Reference to the famous gangsters

Until I switched to the other side, to the other side

It's no surprise I turned you in (oh-oh)

'Cause us traitors never win

This song is full of negatives—no, never, don't, didn't, nothing

I'm in a getaway car

I left you in a motel bar

The speaker got what she wanted from the affair; she was just using him

Put the money in a bag and I stole the keys

The language of criminality to describe how she behaved in a love affair

That was the last time you ever saw me (oh!)

Drivin' the getaway car

chorus repeats

I was ridin' in a getaway car

I was cryin' in a getaway car

I was dyin' in a getaway car

Progression from the neutral to the negative

Said goodbye in a getaway car

Ridin' in a getaway car

I was cryin' in a getaway car

I was dyin' in a getaway car

Said goodbye in a getaway car

GETAWAY CAR

[analysis]

A song that plays with the imagery of gangsters and heists, "Getaway Car" describes a love affair that, like so many in Swift's oeuvre, seemed to be doomed from the beginning. Even the opening line foreshadows the outcome: the contrast between "starts" and "getaway car" (which, after all, usually signals the *end* of a crime) reminds us that something isn't quite right here, as does the song beginning with two negatives ("no, nothing").

There are allusions to Charles Dickens' nineteenth-century work, *A Tale of Two Cities*, to classic cinema like *The Great Escape* (1963), and to real-life gangsters Bonnie and Clyde. The speaker twists these, and other well-known phrases, to illustrate the unconventional nature of the affair, and also the way in which problematic love can have a devastating allure (the "worst of crimes" can still feel like the best of times). There are frequent lines that begin as literal statements then quickly turn into metaphors ("I struck a match and blew your mind"), and this motion from the concrete to the vague might suggest a lack of certainty and commitment that perhaps marred the relationship itself. There's a lot of slant rhyme, which again adds to the sense of incompleteness.

The speaker portrays herself as a criminal carrying out a heist—something Swift does several times on *Reputation*, and also in later songs such as "Vigilante Shit" and "no body no crime." We might also read connections between other Swift tracks: the reference to "X marks the spot" recalls the line in "End Game," "I bury hatchets but I keep maps of where I put 'em," while the mention of a "love story" echoes Swift's song of the same name, from *Fearless*.

The song directly addresses its object ("you"), using imperatives to try and convince him of the speaker's point of view (that he should've known there was no future there). There are also frequent negatives, again accentuating the fact that the relationship was doomed from the beginning. The change of the chorus from "riding" to "crying" and then "dying" at the end reminds the listener of the affair's quick progression into catastrophe, but also fades out sonically—just as a getaway car might fade off into the distance at the end of a film.

Call It What You Want

My **c**astle **c**rumbled overnight

I brought a knife to a gunfight

They took the crown, but it's alright

All the liars are calling me one

Nobody's heard from me for months

I'm doing better than I ever was

Recalls the narrative of "Look What You Made Me Do," alluding to the vitriol directed at Swift in the wake of the Kanye West and Kim Kardashian phone call incident. The bitterness and anger at the beginning of Reputation dissipate by the arrival of this track

Caesura, asking us to wait in suspense

'Cause my baby's fit like a daydream

British slang for good-looking, alluding to the object of this song

Walkin' with his head down, I'm the one he's walkin' to

So call it what you want, yeah, call it what you want to

My baby's fly like a jet stream

Twisting the notion of "fly," meaning cool, to interpret it literally

High above the whole scene, loves me like I'm brand new

Image of renewal goes back to "Clean"

So call it what you want, yeah, call it what you want to

A common Swiftian image. See also "Blank Space" and "Slut!"

All my flowers grew back as thorns

Windows boarded up after the storm

Emotional withdrawal. The image of a house with windows boarded up will recur in "Death By A Thousand Cuts"

He built a fire just to keep me warm

There's a reversal of this idea in "long story short": "now I just keep you warm"

All the drama queens taking swings

All the jokers dressin' up as kings

They fade to nothin' when I look at him

Swift deploys the imagery of a card game, suggesting the frivolity and silliness of the drama

And I know I make the same mistakes every time

Bridges burn, I never learn, at least I did one thing right

I did one thing right

Neat linkage of the double rhyme suggest this is a recurring pattern

I'm **l**aughin' with my **l**over, makin' forts under covers

Trust him like a brother, yeah, you know I did one thing right

Triple rhyme

Swift often uses this image, as in "loml" and "The Smallest Man Who Ever Lived"

Starry eyes sparkin' up my darkest night

chorus repeats

I want to wear his initial

On a chain 'round my neck, chain 'round my neck

Swift seems to want to highlight the different circumstances here versus the necklace from "Out Of The Woods"

Not because he owns me

But 'cause he really knows me

Which is more than they can say, I

See "Dress": "everyone thinks that they know us, but they know nothing"

I recall late November

Holdin' my breath, slowly I said

"You don't need to save me

But would you run away with me?"

This marks an evolution since the days of "Romeo save me" in "Love Story" and sets this relationship apart as remarkable

Yes (would you run away?)

Phrases in parentheses, which sound like echoes, are fitting for a song that discusses rumors and gossip, but also suggests an uncertainty on the part of the speaker that we also see in "Delicate" ("is it cool that I said all that?")

My baby's fit like a daydream

Walkin' with his head down, I'm the one he's walkin' to

(Call it what you want, call it what you want, call it)

So call it what you want, yeah, call it what you want to

My baby's fly like a jet stream

High above the whole scene, loves me like I'm brand new

(Call it what you want, call it what you want, call it)

So call it what you want, yeah, call it what you want to

Call it what you want, yeah, call it what you want

To

The pause before "to" mirrors the reference to the speaker holding her breath in the song's bridge

CALL IT WHAT YOU WANT

[analysis]

This song is very characteristic of *Reputation,* which sees Swift explicitly distance herself from gossip and ostentatiously abandon control over her own narrative (while in fact exerting quite a lot of control, as multiple critics and reviews noted at the time of release). The frequent contrasts in the song's opening emphasize the way in which the speaker has gained a new perspective on difficult events—potentially events alluded to in other tracks from *Reputation*—after falling in love. Significantly, there are signs that this love is of a different nature to those the speaker has experienced before: connections with some of Swift's past songs highlight a development from wanting to be saved ("Love Story," "White Horse") to valuing equality, trust, and intimate shared knowledge. The song alternates between seriousness and playfulness, with its use of slang and innovative metaphors contrasting the violent imagery of weapons and ruins. Most of the lines rhyme, which suggests a neatness and a continuity that perhaps reflect the stability of the relationship that the speaker is discussing.

The "you" of the song alternates between signifying gossips and critics ("call it what **you** want") and the beloved object of the song ("would **you** run away with me"). It's as if we are given tiny glimpses into the intimate world of the speaker and her lover that are then taken away, only for us to be called out on our ability to spread rumors. It's slightly disorienting, which might be a deliberate ploy on the part of the speaker: to refuse us the whole story.

chapter seven

LOVER

The Archer

Metaphor sets us up for a song about emotional pain and risk

Combat, I'm ready for combat

I say I don't want that, but what if I do?

Contradiction establishes wavering uncertainty

'**C**ause **c**ruelty wins in the movies

Questions the reality of what we are sold on the screen

I've got a hundred thrown-out speeches I almost said to you

Swift's work often explores the need to find, or difficulty of finding, the right words

Easy they come, easy they go

I jump from the train, I ride off alone

Fitting with the filmic lyrics and anticipates "The Bolter"

I never grew up, it's getting so old

Help me **h**old onto you

"Old" is used in the sense of tedious and repetitive: staying childlike is no longer a novelty, no longer fun

I've been the archer

I've been the prey

Recalls the Greek myth of Actaeon, the hunter who was turned by the goddess Diana into a deer and pursued by his own hounds. The archer is also a potent symbol, associated with Cupid and his arrows

Who could ever leave me, darling?

But who could stay?

Masochistic image suggesting love is only desirable "when it's torture"

Dark side, I search for your dark side

But what if I'm alright, right, right, right here?

Epizeuxis—as if stuttering to articulate her feelings

And I cut off my nose just to spite my face

Then I hate my reflection for years and years

Metaphor of self-sabotage becomes literal, distorting her reflection and furthering a sense of self-loathing. Anticipates "I'll look directly at the sun but never in the mirror" in "Anti-Hero"

Habitual cycles

I wake in the night, I pace like a ghost

Burning down of the Lover house on the Eras Tour

The room is on fire, invisible smoke

And all of my heroes die all alone

Damage isn't clear until it's too late

Help me hold onto you

I've been the archer

I've been the prey

Screaming, who could ever leave me, darling?

But who could stay?

(I see right through me, I see right through me)

This fits with the "I pace like a ghost" reference above

'Cause they see right through me

They see right through me

They see right through

Can you see right through me?

They see right through

They see right through me

I see right through me

I see right through me

Grammatically, it would be more common to say "myself," but "me" suggests more strongly that the speaker is viewing herself with the eyes of an outside observer

All the king's horses, all the king's men

Couldn't put me together again

Falling apart—the nursery rhyme reference corroborates "I never grew up" above

'Cause all of my enemies started out friends

A poignant line that presses the uncertainty of the future and/or the speaker's potential to sabotage all close relationships

Help me hold onto you

I've been the archer

I've been the prey

Who could ever leave me, darling?

But who could stay?

(I see right through me, I see right through me)

Who could stay?

Who could stay?

Who could stay?

You could stay

You could stay

You

Combat, I'm ready for combat

THE ARCHER

[analysis]

Musically, "The Archer" is interesting because it never peaks in a rousing chorus like so many other Swift songs do. Instead, it hovers on the verge of a climax that never happens, evoking an anxious tension that is evident in the song's lyrics. The major themes of the song are wavering uncertainty, self-loathing, an acknowledgment of previous bad behavior, and a desire to change going forward, so that the speaker might "hold on" to someone. The object of the song is unclear: it might be a lover, but it might also be Swift's audience and fans. It's a song about growing older and wiser and attempting to atone for past bad behavior, which anticipates the revelations we get in "Daylight," the final song on the album.

"The Archer" seems to suggest a realization that we must abandon the scripts we have been sold by "the movies": that real life cannot be lived in reference to films or our "heroes." The uneven rhyme and frequent use of repetition contribute to the feeling that the speaker is working through her emotions as she sings: she often contradicts herself and asks frequent rhetorical questions, highlighting the (self-)doubt at the heart of the song. The contrast between tenses also helps to exemplify this: the song explores how patterns of past behavior influence the present and future, but also the potential to break these patterns. "The Archer" uses familiar Swiftian imagery (hunter and prey, smoke and ghosts) but in different ways to her other works: she is both hunter *and* prey this time; she is haunt*ing*, not haunt*ed*. It's a song of frequent contrasts, the speaker at times determined and resilient, at others desperately vulnerable and afraid. It's no wonder it's track 5 on *Lover*.

The song's title is also a reference to Swift's star sign, Sagittarius.

Miss Americana & The Heartbreak Prince

This is one of Swift's most mysterious and enigmatic songs, leading to a wealth of possible interpretations. Perhaps owing to its discussion of scoreboards and voting, it has been viewed as a political anthem that expresses Swift's disillusionment regarding Republican policies during the American elections, well documented in the Netflix documentary *Miss Americana* (whose title of course hints at a correspondence with this song). It has also been interpreted as a more "straightforward" love song, perhaps addressed to a man who "loves [her] American smile." It might also, of course, be both simultaneously: the depressed damsel seeks solace from the political storm in the arms of her prince.

You know I adore you, I'm crazier for you
Than I was at sixteen, lost in a film scene
Waving homecoming queens, marching band playing
I'm **l**ost in the **l**ights

The breakdown of the rhyme sequences foreshadows the disillusionment and the breakdown of hopes and dreams

Present participle as if we are there, too

American glory faded before me
Now I'm feeling hopeless, ripped up my prom dress
Running through **r**ose thorns, I saw the **s**coreboard
And ran for my life (ah)

Lost youthful optimism or innocence

No **c**ameras **c**atch my pageant smile
I **c**ounted days, I **c**ounted miles
To see you there, to see you there

Faked, brave face

Anaphora—the lengths to which the speaker has gone

If Swift is Miss Americana, the Heartbreak Prince (both parts of the title are examples of antonomasia) might be her lover, but might also represent an America she fears materializing: one characterized by the oppression of women and the prevalence of fake news. The "you" in the song is enigmatic and ambiguous: is Swift addressing a lover, or her fans, or her countrymen? Or, perhaps, all three?

It's been a long time coming, but
Enjambment mirrors the "long time coming" in real time
It's you and me, that's my whole world
They whisper in the hallway, "She's a bad, bad girl" (okay)
Cheered "okay" in the background reminiscent of high school cheerleaders—perhaps sarcastic defiance
A microcosm for America
The whole school is rolling fake dice
The game is rigged
You play stupid games, you win stupid prizes
It's you and me, there's nothing like this
Metaphor for an election if you subscribe to a political interpretation of this song
Miss Americana and The Heartbreak Prince (okay)
We're so sad, we paint the town blue
A negative twist on "paint the town red," meaning to celebrate. The key contrast may suggest a collective reaction to a tense political climate
Voted most likely to run away with you
Alludes to high school superlatives, but also fits the political dimension
My team is losing, **b**attered and **b**ruising
I see the **h**igh fives between the bad guys
Lends weight to the political interpretation, or women ("depressed damsels") in general
Leave with my **h**ead **h**ung, you are the only one
Who seems to care
Contrast with the "American glory." An uneasy reflection of "fake news" or the country's departure from its historical integrity
American stories **b**urning **b**efore me
I'm feeling helpless, the damsels are depressed
Plural play on "damsel in distress." May refer to Swift's anxiety over the stripping away of women's rights or the prevalence of misogyny
Boys will be boys then, where are the wise men?
Phrase associated with toxic masculinity contrasts with "wise men"

The damsel, Miss Americana, seeking refuge in her Heartbreak Prince

Darling, I'm scared (ah)

No **c**ameras **c**atch my muffled cries

Literal or metaphorical? The former suggests gender-based violence, the latter a desperation to be heard. See Swift's 2020 documentary, Miss Americana, in which she describes being pressured out of talking politics as one of the "good girls"

I counted days, I counted miles

To see you there, to see you there

And now the storm is coming, but

Storms as renewal—a cautiously optimistic line

It's you and me, that's my whole world

They whisper in the hallway, "She's a bad, bad girl" (okay)

The whole school is rolling fake dice

You play stupid games, you win stupid prizes

It's you and me, there's nothing like this

Miss Americana and The Heartbreak Prince (okay)

We're so sad, we paint the town blue

Voted most likely to run away with you

This song explores several of the themes prevalent on *Lover*, namely misogyny, double standards, and toxic masculinity. It combines the imagery of medieval romance and chivalry with that of American high school culture to express disillusionment—but it's a disillusionment tempered by the cautious optimism that "someday we're gonna win."

The repetition (anaphora) emphasizes the negative, and the speaker's reluctance (as a depressed damsel, perhaps)

And I don't want you to (go), I don't really wanna (fight)

'Cause nobody's gonna (win), I think you should come home

And I don't want you to (go), I don't really wanna (fight)

'Cause nobody's gonna (win), I think you should come home

And I don't want you to (go), I don't really wanna (fight)

'Cause nobody's gonna (win), just thought you should know

And I'll never let you (go) 'cause I know this is a (fight)

That someday we're gonna (win)

The song suddenly shifts to an optimistic note, surprising after all the negatives in the bridge: the speaker was reluctant to fight but seems to have changed her mind. The negative of "I don't" becomes more positive, about tenacity and determination: "I'll never let you go"

It's you and me, that's my whole world

They whisper in the hallway, "She's a bad, bad girl"

Oh, I just thought you should know (you should know)

It's you and me, there's nothing like this (like this)

Miss Americana and The Heartbreak Prince (okay)

We're so sad, we paint the town blue (paint it blue)

Voted most likely to run away with you

And I don't want you to (go), I don't really wanna (fight)

'Cause nobody's gonna (win), I think you should come home

And I'll never let you (go) 'cause I know this is a (fight)

That someday we're gonna (win), just thought you should know

It's you and me, that's my whole world

They whisper in the hallway, "She's a bad, bad girl"

She's a bad, bad girl

She perhaps accepts the inevitable criticism she might receive for speaking out

In "Miss Americana & The Heartbreak Prince," the use of end rhyme that gradually disintegrates into half rhyme and then no rhyme suggests a steady fragmentation, mirroring the song's angry disillusionment, evident in images like the ripped-up prom dress. The exact object of the disillusionment is unclear, but it certainly seems to involve both America and men behaving badly. However, the litany of negatives in the bridge gives way to a more positive sentiment: we *will* win the fight.

Death By A Thousand Cuts

Saying goodbye is death by a thousand cuts

Originally a grisly execution method, but now used to express something torturously slow and unpleasant

Flashbacks waking me up

I get drunk, but it's not enough

Assonance—mirrors the idea that it's not enough (because the rhyme isn't perfect)

'Cause the morning comes and you're not my baby

I look through the windows of this love

Symbolism of the Lover house

Even though we boarded them up

Chandelier's still flickering here

Love and devotion as a chandelier suggests opulence, but it's only flickering rather than giving a steady light

'Cause I can't pretend it's ok when it's not

It's death by a thousand cuts

I dress to kill my time

A twist on two clichéd idioms that combines them in a new way: putting on a brave face to pass time

I take the long way home

I ask the traffic lights if it'll be all right

They say, "I don't know"

And what once was ours is no one's now

I see you everywhere

The only thing we share

Is this small town

Effectively: she no longer shares anything with her once-beloved

You said it was a great love

One for the ages

Anticipates the line in "the 1": "the greatest loves of all time are over now"

But if the story's over

Why am I still writing pages?

A meta-textual reference—she writes a lot about writing

chorus repeats

My heart, my hips, my body, my love

Asyndeton—the rush of images without connecting conjunctions adds to the flashback

Trying to find a part of me that you didn't touch

Gave up on me like I was a bad drug

Swiftian simile

Now I'm searching for signs in a haunted club

The relationship has left residual traces everywhere

Our songs, our films, united we stand

Our country, guess it was a lawless land

"Our country" used as a metaphor for a relationship—from unity to lawlessness—see also "exile"

Quiet my fears with the touch of your hand

Paper cut stings from our paper thin plans

Potentially an allusion to "Paper Rings," but also a clever reworking of the title

My time, my wine, my spirit, my trust

Trying to find a part of me you didn't take up

The relationship as pervasive through every part of her life

Gave you too much but it wasn't enough

But I'll be all right, it's just a thousand cuts

The "just" here is ironic

chorus repeats

I take the long way home

I ask the traffic lights if it'll be all right

Prosopopoeia—reading signs and symbolism when we experience love and loss. "I don't know" echoes the flickering chandelier

They say, "I don't know"

The song ends on a negative, uncertain statement

There is very little full rhyme in this song. Instead it relies on half rhyme, internal rhyme and assonance to create the feeling of something not quite cohesive, but adrift

DEATH BY A THOUSAND CUTS

[analysis]

This song puns on the idea, common in music and poetry, of a broken heart as a physical wound. Instead of leaving one gaping hole, Swift rethinks the metaphor and suggests that heartbreak is closer to thousands of tiny cuts, easily and painfully reopened through flashbacks and haunting memories. A fading love as something that dies slowly anticipates her later reference in "illicit affairs" to dying "a million little times." She visualizes the imbalance between her lover's presumed feelings and her own via a series of metaphors. The relationship is a house—now boarded up for him, but for *her* the chandelier is still flickering—a country, formerly united, now lawless—and a book—finished, though *she's* still writing. All these metaphors suggest a question that runs through the song: what *is* the best metaphor for a love that has now died? How can one properly express these feelings through language? It's the same struggle we find in "Red." A lack of full rhyme contributes to this sense of uncertainty, as if the speaker is struggling to make things make coherent sense.

The song's bridge makes effective use of asyndeton to suggest the memories and ideas are overwhelming the speaker as she undergoes these flashbacks, desperately trying to find both a physical and emotional "part of me that you didn't touch." Although there's repetition of "my," there is also the sense that these things *aren't* hers anymore, having been irreversibly marked by the object of the song. The song ends on an inconclusive, uncertain statement, which fits its general mood of struggle and confusion.

This song explores different types of light, identifying daylight as the most pure—the relationship to come surpasses all others

Daylight

A previous "era," defined by New York

My love was as cruel as the cities I lived in

Perhaps deliberately ambiguous: the love the speaker bestowed on others or a particular person

Everyone looked worse in the light

Foreshadows the exploration of light as getting to know someone deeply, flaws included

There are so many lines that I've crossed unforgiven

I'll tell you the truth, but never goodbye

I don't wanna look at anything else now that I saw you

I don't wanna think of anything else now that I thought of you

I've been sleeping so long in a twenty-year dark night

And now I see daylight, I only see daylight

Links to "have I known you twenty seconds, or twenty years?" in "Lover"

Luck of the draw only draws the unlucky

Chiasmus here implies the cliché of "luck of the draw" contradicted her actual experience

And so I became the butt of the joke

Wiser hindsight

I wounded the good and I trusted the wicked

Clearing the air, I breathed in the smoke

Paradox similar to the one we find in "Clean." "Smoke" might refer to London as a place and person, as it seems to do in "The Black Dog" and "So Long, London"

Maybe you ran with the wolves and refused to settle down

Maybe I've stormed out of every single room in this town

Threw out our cloaks and our daggers because it's morning now

The two lovers have no more secrets from each other

It's brighter now, now

Plays up dramatic contrast between love before and now

I don't wanna look at anything else now that I saw you

(I can never look away)

I don't wanna think of anything else now that I thought of you

(Things will never be the same)

I've been sleeping so long in a twenty-year dark night

(Now I'm wide awake)

And now I see daylight (Daylight), I only see daylight (Daylight)

I only see daylight, daylight, daylight, daylight

I only see daylight, daylight, daylight, daylight

The repetition, or epizeuxis, here suggests the speaker reveling in this new-found light

And I can still see it all (In my mind)

Flashbacks and memories appearing to the speaker as she sings

All of you, all of me (Intertwined)

I once believed love would be (Black and white)

Monochrome aesthetic of Reputation; love is more nuanced than the speaker had previously imagined

But it's golden (Golden)

And I can still see it all (In my head)

Back and forth from New York (Sneaking in your bed)

Internal half rhyme

I once believed love would be (Burning red)

The explicit callback to "Red" indicates the speaker's growth and development

But it's golden

Like daylight, like daylight

Like daylight, daylight

This color seems to have the same object in Swift's discography, such as "invisible string," "Dancing With Our Hands Tied" and "Dress"

chorus repeats

Like daylight

It's golden like daylight

You gotta step into the daylight and let it go

Just let it go, let it go

Voiceover adds a level of intimacy and spontaneity

I wanna be defined by the things that I love

Not the things I hate

Not the things that I'm afraid of, I'm afraid of

Not the things that haunt me in the middle of the night

Contrast to daylight

I, I just think that

You are what you love

A conscious departure from being haunted by love

DAYLIGHT

[analysis]

"Daylight" makes significant intertextual connections with Swift's other work to construct its main message: that the speaker has never known true, authentic, *real* love until now. Cycling through some of the colors prominently associated with her past albums and "eras," Swift associates these periods with an extended sleep in darkness, compared to the dazzling daylight in which the speaker now finds herself. This "golden" state is linked to the object of the song, possibly the same object as in the songs "Lover," "Dancing With Our Hands Tied," "Dress," "So It Goes," "End Game," and, later, "invisible string," since there are textual connections via the color gold.

There is frequent epizeuxis of the word "daylight," almost to the point of being excessive, which seems to reflect the dizzying, overwhelming quality of the speaker's revelations at finally being "wide awake." Since many of Swift's songs associate romance with the deep hours of the night (as a fan once wrote on Reddit, "2AM is not a good time for blondie"), "Daylight" marks a clear contrast to some of these previous anthems. Contrast is key to this song more generally: it uses structures like chiasmus to oppose the speaker's previous lifestyle and beliefs with her new-found contentment.

In spite of these carefully constructed contrasts, there is also a feeling of spontaneity to the song, achieved through its use of anaphora and repetition but also its parenthetical phrases. These suggest a stream of consciousness as the speaker muses on her past and her present, visited by flashbacks and images in her mind. The closure of the song with a spoken voiceover adds to this intimate feel.

"Daylight" was the original title intended for the album *Lover.*

chapter eight

FOLKLORE

my tears ricochet

This song stemmed from Swift's dispute with Big Machine records, after she felt that her masters had been stolen from her. It seems to allude to the way in which Scott Borchetta, the label's CEO and Swift's mentor, betrayed her trust: Swift noted that, "all of a sudden this person that you trusted more than anyone in the world is the person that can hurt you the most." Swift described the song as narrating "an embittered tormentor showing up at the funeral of his fallen object of obsession," and noted that she had been "triggered" by stories of divorce in the run-up to writing it.

We gather here, we line up

A pronoun that immediately draws the listener in to become part of the narrative

Weepin' in a sunlit room, and

Stark contrast: the incongruity of being somewhere bright while experiencing deep grief

If I'm on fire, you'll be made of ashes too

Cremation—we are hearing from the speaker at her own funeral. But "on fire" also implies a winning streak. This would fit with the revenge elements in the song

Intimate

Even on my worst day, did I deserve, babe

Internal rhyme links the two concepts: she might have deserved this hell

All the hell you gave me?

Answers her own question—no, she didn't deserve it

'Cause I loved you, I swear I loved you

'Til my dying day

Enjambment implies that the speaker is in fact already dead. There are echoes of the novel The Lovely Bones, written from the point of view of a dead girl watching her family's grief unfold

I didn't have it in myself to go with grace

And you're the hero flying around, saving face

Appears to be ironic, the object is no hero

And if I'm dead to you, why are you at the wake?

Cursing my name, wishing I stayed

Look at how my tears ricochet

Double rhyme links the concepts, but it's only half rhyme, suggesting something isn't quite right here

Music critic Eric Mason described the song as "one of *folklore's* most straightforwardly resentful stories." Unsurprisingly, it's track 5 on the album. It is awash with gothic, funereal imagery but plays on the idea of death as both literal and metaphorical, suggesting that the naive, trusting past self of the speaker has died and that she has been reborn as a bitter, ghostly figure.

We gather stones, never knowing what they'll mean
Some to throw, some to make a diamond ring
You know I didn't want to **h**ave to **h**aunt you
But what a ghostly scene
You wear the same jewels that I gave you
As you bury me

Gathering stones is a funereal image, but also suggests gathering evidence to be used against someone

The speaker was once prized by the object, or perhaps a reference to one of Swift's albums

The speaker steps outside of herself, as if she is observing the funeral from afar

Betrayal, but also the object is truly unable to forget the speaker

I didn't have it in myself to go with grace
'Cause when I'd fight, you used to tell me I was brave
And if I'm dead to you, why are you at the wake?
Cursing my name, wishing I stayed
Look at how my tears ricochet

Poignant: the object once had a caring, almost parental relationship with the speaker

And I can go anywhere I want
Anywhere I want, just not home
And you can aim for my heart, go for blood
But you would still miss me in your bones
And I still talk to you (when I'm **s**creaming at the **sk**y)

Tragic—the speaker is caught in a liminal state and is not free at all

Violent imagery that underscores a destructive relationship

Funereal

She only talks to him in an angry monologue, alone

Potentially a reference to Swift's masters, sold without her consent. The unsettling line implies the object of the song cannot be soothed by these songs, since they were illegitimately acquired

And when you can't sleep at night (you hear my stolen lullabies)

The song draws on the language of masochistic, toxic relationships: of love as pain and the repeated seeking of conflict, but in a way that is much more sinister than songs like "Blank Space," which uses similar ideas. The frequent internal rhyme and assonance, and devices like polyptoton, create parallels between the speaker and the object of the song, which reinforces the idea of a troubling obsession and an irrepressible yet destructive connection between the two of them.

I didn't have it in myself to go with grace

A central image in which both parties lose, but the pain recedes with time

And so the battleships will sink beneath the waves

You had to kill me, but it killed you just the same

Cursing my name, wishing I stayed

Polyptoton—they will forever will be inextricably linked

You turned into your worst fears

Liberal way in which the object tries to blame anyone but himself

And you're tossing out blame, drunk on this pain

Recalls "I get drunk on jealousy" from "Blank Space," but without the light-heartedness

Crossing out the good years

And you're cursing my name, wishing I stayed

Look at how my tears ricochet

This rebirth of the ghostly figure has also engendered violence: "ricochet" is an interesting word choice more commonly used for the action of a bullet bouncing off a hard surface. The imagery evokes gunfire, collateral damage, revenge, and weaponized grief on the part of the speaker. There is also the sense that the bullet/tears have not yet found their intended target—or, perhaps, that they have wounded *more* than their intended target. The central image is fundamentally paradoxical, since tears of course cannot physically wound, but its metaphorical aspect reflects Swift's oft-noted ability to use songwriting as a means of enacting revenge and working through difficult emotions.

invisible string

Anastrophe to foreground the colors

Green was the color of the **gr**ass

Nashville, Tennessee

Where I used to read at Centennial Park

I used to think I would meet somebody there

Teal was the color of your shirt

Assonance in "teal" and "green" suggest the invisible string connecting the speaker and the object

When you were sixteen at the yogurt shop

You used to work at to make a little money

Time as a mischievous entity

Time, curious time

Gave me no compasses, gave me no signs

Swift frames time as someone who might guide her through space

Were there clues I didn't see?

And isn't it just so pretty to think

Allusion to the last line of Ernest Hemingway's The Sun Also Rises

All along there was some

Invisible string

Allusion to Charlotte Brontë's Jane Eyre: "I have a strange feeling with regard to you. As if I had a string somewhere under my left ribs, tightly knotted to a similar string in you."

Tying you to me?

1989 Bad was the blood of the song in the cab

On your first trip to LA

You ate at my favorite spot for dinner

Bold was the waitress on our three year trip

Getting **l**unch down by the **l**akes

She said I looked like an American singer

Time, mystical time

Cuttin' me open, then healin' me fine

Were there clues I didn't see?

And isn't it just so pretty to think

All along there was some

Invisible string

Tying you to me?

Ooh

A string that pulled me *Fated—the string has agency*

Out of all the wrong arms right into that dive bar *"Delicate" begins with "dive bar on the East side"*

Something wrapped all of my past mistakes in barbed wire

Protection. In "tolerate it," Swift uses blankets over barbed wire as a metaphor for solace

Chains around my demons, wool to brave the seasons

Love providing resilience

One single thread of gold tied me to you

True love as golden, as in "Daylight"

Cold was the steel of my axe to grind *Metaphor of anger rendered literal*

For the **b**oys who **b**roke my heart

Now I send their babies presents

Gold was the color of the leaves

When I showed you around Centennial Park

Hell was the journey but it brought me **h**eaven *With hindsight, how pain helps us become the person we are today*

Time, wondrous time

Gave me the blues and then **p**urple **p**ink skies *Sadness, but the whole line reflects the aesthetic of Lover, suggesting that this song is about the same muse*

And it's cool, baby, with me

And isn't it just so pretty to think

All along there was some

Invisible string

Tying you to me?

INVISIBLE STRING

[analysis]

This song features quite a few "invisible strings" of its own, in the form of allusions to both classic literature and Swift's other writing. It draws on Ernest Hemingway and Charlotte Brontë, as well as Swift songs such as "Bad Blood," "Delicate," and "the lakes." It also references real places, such as Centennial Park in Nashville, the Lake District, and Swift's favorite restaurant in LA. One of Swift's most intertextual songs, it weaves together multiple strands into a meditation upon subtle connections only recognizable with hindsight, and it questions the existence and operations of fate. Every relationship is formed from the invisible strings of past connections and feelings, Swift seems to suggest, just as every song also draws on past influences.

There is frequent use of end rhyme, which lends the song a neat, cohesive feel that mirrors the way in which everything seems to be falling perfectly into place. The enjambment adds to the feel of it flowing, unimpeded, like the time that is a central theme—even a character. It's a song that is rich in color—emphasized by anastrophe—which also links it to Swift's album *Lover*, suggesting a common muse for both works. Gold is the color that features most heavily, and it is the one that Swift identified with true love in "Daylight." There's also frequent use of contrasts—cutting and healing, hell and heaven—to emphasize the necessity of learning from painful past experience in order to get to where one is now, a favorite theme in Swift's music. "invisible string" seems to show Swift looking back at her past experience and past writing, and recognizing with delight the intricate connections between them all—something that she has also trained her fans to do since the beginning of her career.

seven

Please **pi**cture me *Alliteration amplifies the plea*

In the trees *Environmentalist Jeff Opperman noted that Swift uses nature-related words seven (!) times more than other artists*

I hit my peak at seven

Feet in the swing

Over the creek *Assonance in "ee" means we expect Swift to sing "seventeen," but the revelation is that the speaker feels she peaked much younger*

I was too scared to jump in

But I, I was high in the sky *Quadruple internal rhyme—dreamy feeling that captures the elation of looking down at the world from above, as in peaking*

With Pennsylvania under me

Are there still beautiful things? *Fittingly, "sylvania" comes from the Latin for "trees" or "wood"*

Perhaps a nod to her country music roots

Sweet tea in the summer

Cross your heart, won't tell no other *Evokes the secret pacts of childhood*

And though I can't recall your face

I still got love for you

Your braids like a pattern *Sometimes we only remember random flashes from our childhood and not necessarily the most "important" details*

Love you to the moon and to Saturn

Passed down like folk songs *A somewhat meta element. This song is, in itself, passing down the emotions described in it as if they were folk songs*

The love lasts so long

Double rhyme of "folk songs" and "so long" emphasizes the power to immortalize

And I've been meaning to tell you

I think your house is haunted

Your dad is always mad and that must be why *Dramatic irony—the listener knows the anger is rooted in an adult world, not a supernatural one*

And I think you should come live with

Childhood innocence

Me and we can be pirates

Make-believe, but pirates can defend themselves

Then you won't have to cry

Or hide in the closet *Hidden homosexuality or queerness. The speaker's friend must hide certain aspects of herself, or to literally escape her angry father*

And just like a folk song

Our love will be passed on

More specific than "the love" earlier, and perhaps suggests a queer reading. This song is indeed passing on the love between these two characters

Please **p**icture me

In the weeds *Objective correlative: the weeds symbolically mirroring the emotions discussed in the verse*

Before I learned civility *A somewhat sad reminder that wild freedom is eradicated out of children*

I used to scream ferociously

Assonance

Any time I wanted

I, I *In a Freudian reading, the focus on "I" evokes the way in which a child is focused on their "id" or basic desires*

Sweet tea in the summer

Cross my heart, won't tell no other

And though I can't recall your face

I still got love for you *Practicality and innocence in this combination. The sweater also alludes to one of the key symbols of folklore: a "cardigan"*

Pack your dolls and a sweater

We'll move to India forever

Recalls Frances Hodgson Burnett's children's novel, A Little Princess

Passed down like folk songs

Our love lasts so long

"So long" also as a farewell

Frequent rhyme in the chorus is reminiscent of simple childhood songs

SEVEN

[analysis]

We might read in "seven" echoes of British Romantic poet William Wordsworth's poem "Ode: Intimations of Immortality from Recollections of Early Childhood," in which the speaker muses upon the glorious innocence and freedom of childhood that disappears as we grow up. It features the famous line, "shades of the prison-house begin to close upon the growing boy." Swift explores a similar idea in this song, which posits childhood as an idyllic "peak" whose delights and liberties are steadily curtailed by the onset of adulthood, a theme she had explored previously ("Never Grow Up," "Innocent") and would revisit later ("Robin"). There are several lines in the song that sound like they are uttered by a naive child, and the rhyme of the chorus recalls childhood playground chants. However, there's also the sense that the song is being narrated by the speaker's present, older self, who mourns the freedom she left behind. A particularly poignant example is the reference to the haunted house: the speaker suggests, wistfully, that it was much easier to believe in supernatural forces as a child than to acknowledge, with the hindsight of adulthood, patterns of possible parental abuse. With her repeated injunction to the listener to picture her, peaking, at seven, the speaker expresses a nostalgic desire to return to those times. Since she cannot, she will, at the very least, immortalize them through language.

The setting is typically folklorian, with the images of treetops and weeds used to mirror the wildness and freedom of the child. The references to folk songs fit with the album's main concept and also constitute an example of meta commentary: this song is, itself, a folk song that keeps the love of these two figures alive.

this is me trying

I've been having a hard time adjusting

I had the shiniest wheels, now they're rusting *The superlative distinguishes the contrast—implies the speaker was once going places and is now stuck*

I didn't know if you'd care if I came back

I have a lot of regrets about that

Pulled the car off the road to the lookout *Hindsight*

They have veered off course

Could've followed my fears all the way down *Suicidal ideation—the fears have agency*

And maybe I don't quite know what to say

But I'm here in your doorway *A liminal space of hesitation or significant transition. Like the speaker in "betty," the speaker is unsure if he or she will be granted admittance*

I just wanted you to know

That this is me trying *The speaker's whole state of being is one of trying, potentially in multiple different ways*

A gesture to right past wrongs

I just wanted you to know

That this is me trying

They told me all of my cages were mental *A frequent Swiftian symbol of self-sabotage and/or being held back by one's beliefs or mental illness*

Combines two idioms

So I got wasted like all my potential

And my words shoot to kill when I'm mad

The speaker using words as weapons in anger

I have a lot of regrets about that

I was so ahead of the curve, the curve became a sphere *Being precocious or advanced in one's youth might backfire. The curve has the agency over this trajectory*

Fell behind on my classmates, and I ended up here

Pouring out my heart to a stranger *Extends the metaphor: fell off or moved so far ahead on the sphere the speaker ended up behind*

But I didn't pour the whiskey

Antanaclasis—the metaphorical "pour" is preferable to the literal

I just wanted you to know

That this is me trying

I just wanted you to know

That this is me trying

At least I'm trying

And it's hard to be at a party when I feel like an open wound

It's hard to be anywhere these days when all I want is you

You're a flashback in a film reel on the one screen in my town

And I just wanted you to know

That this is me trying

(And maybe I don't quite know what to say)

I just wanted you to know

That this is me trying

At least I'm trying

Anaphora here puts "this is me trying" into greater context: it is braver given its difficulty

The speaker feels raw and vulnerable around others, but an open wound may also cause others to recoil

"My town" may be a metaphor for the speaker herself. Life is small and restricted due to the aforementioned "mental cages"

Parenthetical adds a layer of framing here: the listener is encouraged to hear the speaker while bearing in mind that she doesn't necessarily feel these are the right words

Uncertain note that could either be self-doubt, or defensiveness. It implies a response from the object of the song that the listener is not privy to

THIS IS ME TRYING

[analysis]

“this is me trying” relies on several simple but resonant images and offers some of Swift’s cleverest wordplay. It seems to narrate the apology and confession of a speaker who has strayed from the path they (and others) had envisaged for themselves earlier in life, going “off the rails” in their youth (due to those shiny wheels rusting) and descending into alcoholism and self-sabotage. It explores weighty themes such as mental illness, suicidal ideation, and addiction, all the while suggesting that the speaker hasn’t quite found the right words. This might read as somewhat ironic, since the song manifests clever, fitting metaphors such as the curve becoming a sphere, a succinct but original way of alluding to the ways in which youthful precocity might be a double-edged sword, something that Swift has alluded to experiencing personally. Indeed, Swift has said the song was inspired by her feelings of “being worth absolutely nothing” in 2016 and 2017, following her “cancellation” on social media.

Swift's use of puns and antanaclasis fit with the song's theme of words being difficult: they frequently have double meanings, perhaps indicating the speaker's struggle to pin them down and fully express herself. "this is me trying" might, then, refer to the speaker's trying to make language work for her, to fully encompass her mental, physical, and emotional difficulties. Swift has bemoaned her need to always "have the last word, in public and private," perhaps one of the reasons this song considers both the damage words can do and their ability to trip us up. There's a lot riding on getting those words right, since the speaker is trying to articulate serious regrets and also to make up for what seems to be years of difficult behavior, including wounding with words. This might also be the reason that the song's chorus is very simple and spare, simply repeating two lines: the speaker gives up trying to make excuses and strips things back to the essentials: her most vulnerable, authentic self.

hoax

This first verse follows a very strict meter and rhyme pattern: the images all pertain to the object of the song

My only one
My smoking gun
My eclipsed sun
This has broken me down
My twisted knife
My sleepless night
My win-less fight
This has frozen my ground

Implies damage recently caused to the speaker, but potentially self-inflicted

Happiness replaced with darkness, or the object is so important he can eclipse everything else

Passive = powerless

Who is wielding the knife? Element of sadism, or masochism, or both

Coining her own compound adjective, getting to the bare bones of the idea in a way that more complex words might not

Anaphora of "my" is curious: she is claiming ownership of images with negative connotations

Metaphor for a heart made cold by grief or despair

Stood on the cliffside
Screaming, "Give me a reason"
Your faithless love's the only hoax
I believe in
Don't want no other shade of blue
But you
No other sadness in the world would do

She's not just standing in ~~quiet~~ contemplation of the view, but in distress

This love is fundamentally false, a carefully crafted deception

Infidelity or a love that lacks conviction

"Hoax" vs. "I believe" = self-sabotage

Blue characterizes this specific muse

The speaker is challenging the object to give her a reason to jump, or in fact a reason not to. The sibilance here is slightly unsettling, perhaps evoking the rushing wind as she stands on the cliff

Embracing the trials that come with loving this object

My best laid plan
Your sleight of hand
My barren land
I am ash from your fire

Hostile landscape or infertility: He/it has turned her into a wasteland devoid of creativity and inspiration

Fire is typical of passion in Swift's lyrics. Instead the line evokes "ashes to ashes"—this love has killed her

chorus repeats

You know I left a part of me back in New York
You knew the hero died, so what's the movie for?

Has the speaker finally gone the same way as her heroes, as she once feared in "The Archer"?

You knew it still hurts underneath my scars *The pain will never heal*

From when they pulled me apart

You knew the password, so I let you in the door *Vulnerability*

You knew you won, so what's the point of keeping score? *Not only suggests the speaker's complete surrender, but that the object is vindictive and calculating*

You knew it still hurts underneath my scars *Anaphora of "you knew" echoes "willow": "the more that you say, the less I know," and suggests an uneven power dynamic*

From when they pulled me apart

But what you did was just as dark

Darling, this was just as hard *Ambiguous, but alludes to a betrayal of the speaker's vulnerabilities by the object*

As when they pulled me apart

My only one

My kingdom come undone *"Kingdom come" is a Biblical allusion to heaven, but shattered—similar to the wrecking of the "best laid plan"*

My broken drum *A silencing or muffling of the speaker*

You have beaten my heart *Plays on the above line: "Beaten" as percussion, as winning, as violence, as a heartbeat*

Don't want no other shade of blue

But you

No other sadness in the world would do

HOAX

[analysis]

"hoax" contains some of Swift's most imagery-laden and ambiguous lyrics. It took her over a year to perform it during the acoustic set at the Eras Tour, which fans speculated was possibly because it is one of her darkest songs, hinting as it does at suicidal ideation and domestic violence. It relies on a series of brief images that center around juxtapositions, framing the object of the song as a paradox the speaker struggles to comprehend. At the heart of the song is a highly uneven balance of power: the speaker a passive loser of a battle that the object of the song won long ago, yet her loss and humiliation continue.

While there are certainly unnerving elements in this song that suggest a highly toxic relationship, "hoax" might also allude to the difficulties of opening oneself up to new love when one has been left on one's guard by past trauma. The reference to being pulled apart previously, which has left pain even under scars, and "this" being "just as hard," suggests that the speaker has had to revisit that old pain and trauma in making herself vulnerable to new love—love that comes with its own complications (the object's "sadness"). It might suggest that the object of the song has urged her to revisit her past in order to fully heal, and that this has made the speaker feel so vulnerable it was akin to being beaten, frozen, and burned all over again. The line "you have beaten my heart" suggests that he has finally won, that she has opened up fully, but also suggests physical violence *and* a heartbeat, alluding perhaps to CPR. The theme of death runs through the song, but with the possibility of resurrection, too: that only in symbolically "dying," leaving one's old self and hurt behind, can we rise anew from barren ashes to new love. It's an idea that suggests the mythological phoenix, which Swift later invokes in "You're Losing Me."

the lakes

This song alludes heavily to the Romantic poets, several of whom were inspired by the English Lake District

Is it romantic how all my elegies eulogize me?

I'm not cut out for all these cynical clones

These hunters with cell phones

The Romantics didn't go there to die, but perhaps indicates transformation. Swift's writing is a frequent act of death and reincarnation

Take me to the Lakes where all the poets went to die

Ode

I don't belong, and my beloved, neither do you

Those Windermere peaks look like a **p**erfect **p**lace to cry

British Romantics saw poetry as fueled by "emotion recollected in tranquility"

I'm setting off, but not without my muse

What should **b**e over **b**urrowed under my skin

In **h**eart-stopping waves of **h**urt

Journey, career

I've come too far to watch some namedropping sleaze

Tell me what are my Wordsworth

A pun that references Romantic poet William Wordsworth. It also alludes to the purchase of Swift's masters by Scooter Braun in 2019

chorus repeats

Auroras are uncommon in Britain, and the Romantics were not known for prose. The speaker yearns for an ideal that doesn't match reality

I want auroras and sad prose

I want to watch wisteria grow right over my bare feet

'Cause I haven't moved in years

Foreshadowing here of evermore's "right where you left me," except this stasis is framed as positive

And I want you right here

A red rose grew up out of ice frozen ground

Blossoming of love out of disaster

With no one around to tweet it

Juxtaposition of nature and technology

While I bathe in cliffside pools

With my calamitous love and insurmountable grief

Emotionally significant—washing away negative emotions or experiences

Take me to the Lakes where all the poets went to die

I don't belong, and my beloved, neither do you

Those Windermere peaks look like a perfect place to cry

I'm setting off, but not without my muse

No, not without you

We see anxiety that she may have peaked too soon, as in "seven." A retreat to physical peaks for contemplation and solace

THE LAKES

[analysis]

This song explicitly links the tone and mood of *folklore* with the British Romantic poets, whose influence we can see on the whole album: the juxtaposition of modernity and technology with timeless nature; a desire to escape into simple, rustic life and anonymity; poetic odes dedicated to an inspirational muse. Swift contrasts the cynicism and sleaze of modern technology and social media with an implicitly more authentic life and self that, she hopes, can be achieved by retreating into nature. This also holds true for her romantic (as opposed to Romantic) life: the metaphor of the rose blossoming out of icy ground away from the predatory gaze of cell phones or social media alludes to the possibility of cultivating authentic love only through privacy, something she has learned the hard way since penning songs like "I Know Places." The image of bathing in cliffside pools suggests renewal; a fresh start achieved through flight with her muse.

If we read this song autobiographically, the opening question—is it romantic?—suggests Swift's own cynicism and doubt at what she is becoming within the world of celebrity. It implies the speaker to be in the midst of an identity crisis of sorts, worrying that she has become navel-gazing and self-obsessed, constantly eulogizing herself and questioning her worth. It might be romantic, but it's not Romantic, and the latter is what the speaker seems to crave: she frames escape to the lakes (Lake District) as the only means of reparation. However, the lakes also resurface in the song "invisible string," where a waitress tells her she looks like an "American singer"—this connection implies that Swift is never able to escape her fame completely (she does not, in fact, know places she won't be found).

Swift takes inspiration from the Romantic poets, whose poetry we tend to associate with powerful, spontaneous feeling: the song is full of references to exaggerated emotion, and also to the idea of not belonging, which is very common in Swift's work. There is a quiet tragedy about this song and the speaker's desperate search for a place where she belongs, an urge we can trace back to Swift's debut album ("A Place in This World," "The Outside").

chapter nine

EVERMORE

tolerate it

Parallels with Daphne du Maurier's novel Rebecca

I sit and watch you reading with your

Head low

I **w**ake and **w**atch you breathing with your

Eyes closed

She observes; he doesn't notice

I sit and watch you

And notice everything you do or don't do

Caesura before the second "I" keeps listener in suspense, mirroring how the song's object holds the speaker in suspense as she waits for his attention

You're so much older and wiser and I

Superlatives describe the song's object; the speaker feels belittled in comparison

I wait by the door like I'm just a kid

"I" emphasizes that the speaker's feelings are the focus of the song—and yet not the focus of her lover

Use my best colors for your portrait

In Rebecca, the narrator dresses like her husband's favorite portrait to try to impress him

Lay the table with the fancy shit

And watch you tolerate it

Less childlike and more like an angry woman who recognizes that her worth is not appreciated

If it's all in my head tell me now

Pleading ultimatum

Tell me I've got it wrong somehow

I know my love should be celebrated

The seed of doubt is already sown—celebrated by someone else

But you tolerate it

Love as war anticipates the later dagger—placed there by this "battle hero" who is not much of a hero after all

I greet you with a battle hero's welcome

I take your indiscretions all in good fun

Ironic, bitter

I sit and listen

I **p**olish **p**lates until they **gl**eam and **gl**isten

Double alliteration hints at the monotony. Like "fancy shit" earlier, it implies a bored housewife

You're so much older and wiser and I

chorus repeats

Hints at infidelity, as relationships are built together. To build others without her is the ultimate betrayal

While you were out building other worlds, where was I?

Where's that man who'd throw blankets over my barbed wire?

Echoes "invisible string." Implies he's no longer blanketing her barbed wire, leaving her sharp and dangerous

I made you my temple, my mural, my sky

Now I'm begging for footnotes in the story of your life

Unevenness—the speaker is merely incidental to him

Drawing hearts in the byline

Always taking up too much space or time

Asyndeton and tricolon—rapid emphasis on how pervasive and important he was to her

You assume I'm fine

Anticipates "I know my pain is such an imposition" from "You're Losing Me"

But what would you do if I, I

Break free and leave us in ruins

Destruction of relationship houses is significant in Swift's work, as with the burning of the *Lover* house on the Eras Tour

Took this dagger in me and removed it

Gain the weight of you then lose it

Echoes "All Too Well:" "I'm a soldier who's returning half her weight." It's literalizing the idea of a difficult relationship as a burden

Believe me, I could do it

Shift to a threat rather than a depressed meditation

If it's all in my head tell me now

Tell me I've got it wrong somehow

I know my love should be celebrated

But you tolerate it

I sit and watch you

Vaguely threatening. The speaker is biding her time

TOLERATE IT

[analysis]

One of the many songs on *evermore* that focus on adultery and unhappy relationships, "tolerate it"—track 5—uses a series of metaphors to describe the way in which the object of the poem makes the speaker feel: childlike, stabbed, burdened, bored, neglected, and, of course, merely tolerated. Swift was inspired by Daphne du Maurier's novel, *Rebecca,* and the way in which the narrator's husband "just tolerates her," despite her repeated attempts to impress him. The fundamental contrast in the poem is between the speaker knowing her worth, and recognizing that it's not appreciated by her lover: the repeated "I" and "but" emphasize this, as does the repeated rhyme between the contrasting "celebrated" and "tolerate it." The slightly dreamy, powerful way Swift sings "I" in the song, pausing before the chorus, also hint at the empowerment to come in the finale, as the speaker recognizes her ability to break free and seems to be biding her time. Repeated imperatives enact the "begging" she refers to, but there's a sense that this begging is futile: she already knows it won't work. The speaker's likening of herself to a child reflects several references to age differences in relationships in Swift's oeuvre, such as in "All Too Well" and "Would've, Could've, Should've."

"tolerate it" revisits the Swiftian trope of expressing a relationship using the metaphor of a coauthored book or story, but twists that idea slightly to imply the unevenness of the relationship: this is *not* a coauthored story, but one in which the speaker is merely a footnote, or even a passive reader, able only to doodle in the margins rather than meaningfully contribute. Interestingly, the song is full of references to creative acts—painting and building—as if to suggest that the speaker's creativity could be stifled by the neglect and monotony she experiences at the hands of her lover; she must break free before this happens (this does *not* happen in *Rebecca;* Swift seems to envisage a different ending for her protagonist and a desire to rewrite the story).

happiness

The oppositions in "happiness" perfectly encapsulate the bittersweet, poignant, confused aftermath of a love affair. Facts are distorted by fury, a smile has become a smirk, and a love will no longer last a lifetime.

Honey, when I'm above the trees

Evokes seeing "the forest for the trees," and also echoes the speaker being literally above the trees in "seven"

I see this for what it is

But now I'm right down in it

All the years I've given

Is just shit we're dividing up

Slightly startling after the tender opening of the song

Showed you all of my hiding spots

One of Swift's many images used to depict making oneself vulnerable to a new lover (or friend)

I was dancing when the music stopped

Dancing as a romantic metaphor—as in "Dancing With Our Hands Tied," "How Did It End?" and "loml"

And in the disbelief

I can't face reinvention

I haven't met the new me yet

Poignant given Swift's dexterity with reinvention. The speaker is torn between the old love and the new future

There is a raw, unfiltered, confessional feel to it, achieved by the relative lack of repetition (there isn't the usual verse-chorus-bridge-chorus structure), the use of profanity amid otherwise poetic language, and the way in which the speaker interrupts and contradicts herself (anacoluthon).

The song takes the listener on a journey with the speaker, from confused rage to forgiveness and acceptance, encapsulating in microcosm the mental and emotional progression (and relapse) that follows the end of a relationship.

There'll be happiness after you

But there was happiness because of you

Both of these things can be true

Rhyme sequence breaks down after these lines, giving way to fragmented rhymes and (emotions)

There is happiness *Exists in the present as an abstract concept*

Past the **bl**ood and **b**ruise

Past the **c**urses and **c**ries

Alliteration and plosive sounds make the words harsher

Beyond the terror in the nightfall

Haunted by the look in my eyes

That would've **l**oved you for a **l**ifetime

Leave it all behind *Syntax is ambiguous. Is this an imperative? If so, to whom? Herself? Us? The object of the song?*

And there is happiness *Where? To whom does it belong?*

The song explores the idea of hindsight, reflecting on past wrongs, and acknowledging one's own culpability in a relationship breakdown, doing so through metaphors drawn from the natural world (trees, rain, sunrise) which fit with the semantic landscape of *evermore*. A key theme is that of vulnerability: the pain and anger one feels after opening up physically and emotionally to someone, only for that to fade into the mundanity of dividing up personal possessions.

Intimate address, but this time she is demanding answers. Progression from tender to bitter and questioning

Tell me, when did your winning **sm**ile

Begin to look like a **sm**irk?

Alliteration makes this comparison more jarring

When did all our lessons start to look like weapons pointed at my deepest hurt?

I hope she'll be a beautiful fool

"Beautiful fool" may be a reference to *The Great Gatsby,* by F. Scott Fitzgerald. Daisy says about her daughter, "I hope she'll be a fool—that's the best thing a girl can be in this world, a beautiful little fool." In this song, it's bitter and dismissive, implying that her ex-lover's next girlfriend will be style over substance. We see this line return later, perhaps suggesting that the beautiful fool is the "new me."

Who takes my spot next to you

Echoes "The Story of Us"

No, I didn't mean that

Raw, confessional style; creates an unreliable narrator

Sorry, I can't see **f**acts through all of my **f**ury

You haven't met the new me yet

Subtle change from "I" to "you": the song now considers the object's point of view

There'll be happiness after me

But there was happiness because of me

Both of these things I believe

There is happiness

In our history

Across our great divide

There is a glorious sunrise

Good things to come

Dappled with the flickers of light

From the dress I wore at midnight

"Dappled" has pleasant connotations, implying that past relationships can leave positive marks

Leave it all behind

And there is happiness

Uneven line lengths and sporadic rhyme contribute to the spontaneous feel of the song, which is anchored by the repetition of "happiness": despite some of the tragedy revealed by the lyrics, particularly in references to blood and bruises, the overarching message is one that is quietly positive: a reminder of past, present, and future happiness, in its many varied forms.

I can't make it go away by making you a villain

I guess it's the price I pay for seven years in heaven

Another hint at an unreliable narrator (and perhaps a warning not to interpret all Swift's songs as truthful or autobiographical)

And I pulled your body into mine every goddamn night now I get fake niceties

Barely-suppressed rage emerging

Lengthy line creates an unfiltered, emotional monologue, but also makes the contrast between "then" and "now" even more jarring

No one teaches you what to do

When a good man hurts you

And you know you hurt him too

A climactic moment: the end rhyme neatly captures the realization that they are both at fault

Honey, when I'm above the trees

I see it for what it is

But now my eyes leak acid rain

Her tears are corrosive, hinting at her ability to channel her rage into songs that will make a villain of him and thus harm him in some way

On the pillow where you used to lay your head

Recalls "there's an indentation in the shape of you" in "Dress." It's a physical, tangible legacy left by the departure of a beloved

After giving you the best I had

Tell me what to give after that

A plea, genuinely seeking guidance on what to do with her "best"

All you want from me now

Is the green light of forgiveness

You haven't met the new me yet

And I think she'll give you that

A play on words: the speaker's new self, or the "new her," in the sense of her replacement (the "beautiful fool")?

There'll be happiness after you

But there was happiness because of you too

The "too" indicates a realization that this is not the paradox it seemed to be

Both of these things can be true

There is happiness

In our history

Across our great divide

There is a glorious sunrise

Dappled with the flickers of light

From the dress I wore at midnight

Leave it all behind

Oh, leave it all behind

Leave it all behind

A tricolon (repetition) that emphasizes the ending note of acceptance and forgiveness

And there is happiness

An abstract statement that suits the uncertainty of the song and its hopeful end

There is the comforting prospect of renewal and reinvention: the speaker isn't "the new me" yet, but it is implied that she *will* undergo this transformation. There's also a play on words: "the new her" alludes both to the transformation the speaker will undergo, but also the fact that she recognizes she is replaceable. This double meaning reflects the overall spirit of the poem: one of contradiction and confusion, but also, ultimately, comfort.

coney island

Break my soul in two *Arresting, but ambiguous—is it an imperative or does the speaker mean "I break"?*

Looking for you but you're right here

If I can't relate to you anymore *Caesura (in the way the song is sung)*

Then who am I related to? *Subtle repetition with variation to make us think more deeply about what it means to "relate"*

Opposition

And if this is the long haul

How'd we get here so soon?

Did I close my fist around something delicate? *Violent* *Possible link to "Delicate"*

Did I shatter you? *The fourth rhetorical question in eight lines. Alludes to "champagne problems:" "your heart was glass, I dropped it"*

And I'm sitting on a bench in Coney Island wondering where did my baby go?

The fast times, the bright lights, the merry go *Contrast between the entertainment aspects of Coney Island and the sadness of the speaker*

Sorry for not making you my centerfold

Over and over *The relationship breakdown has been ongoing*

Lost again with no surprises *Foreshadowing the reference to the birthday cake*

Disappointments, close your eyes *Ambiguous syntax: a facial expression of being disappointed, or an imperative?*

And it gets colder and colder

When the sun goes down *The sun setting on the relationship*

The question pounds my head *Unusually violent verb to suggest emotional struggle*

"What's a lifetime of achievement?"

If I pushed you to the edge

But you were too polite to leave me

And do you miss the rogue *A curious, mild word choice for this villain*

Who coaxed you into paradise and left you there? *One should be happy in paradise, but the speaker is no longer there*

Will you forgive my soul

Forgiveness of one's entire being

When you're too wise to trust me and too old to care?

'Cause we were like the mall before the Internet

Grounded in a millennial upbringing and fits the capitalist symbolism of Coney Island

It was the one place to be

Lighthearted language contrasts with themes of guilt and grief

The mischief, the gift wrapped suburban dreams

Bathetic against implied success of "podium" later

Sorry for not winning you an arcade ring

Frames the speaker's lack of devotion in underwhelming material terms

chorus repeats

Were you waiting at our old spot

In the tree line by the gold clock

Symbolic awareness of the neglect

Did I leave you hanging every single day?

Were you standing in the hallway

With a big cake, happy birthday

Envisions a letdown

Did I paint your bluest skies the darkest gray?

A universe away

And when I got into the accident

Flashback

The sight that flashed before me was your face

But when I walked up to the podium

I think that I forgot to say your name

Suggests a (partly) autobiographical reading

chorus repeats

The sight that flashed before me was your face

When the sun goes down

But I think that I forgot to say your name

Over and over

Threads lines from random verses together, as if losing the thread of the conversation. It also summons deathbed imagery

Sorry for not making you my

Making you my

Making you my centerfold

CONEY ISLAND

[analysis]

Perhaps one of Swift's saddest songs about a breakdown in communication, "coney island" juxtaposes the imagery of "suburban dreams" and glittering entertainment with gray loneliness and abandonment. The language alternates between violent verbs of destruction and more gentle sentiments, reflecting the guilt of the speaker for hurting someone for whom he or she still cares very much. There are frequent contrasts, as if to emphasize the promising future (the "long haul") of the couple and how quickly it disintegrated into misunderstanding, resentment, and disappointment. The alluring image of capitalist suburbia perhaps reflects the childlike innocence of the couple in their early days, before all disintegrated into coldness and loneliness. The song is a duet, featuring the vocals of Matt Berninger, which suggests that we hear the story from both perspectives. Each party feels guilty and responsible for abandoning the other, adding to the overall impression of broken communication—even when they are singing simultaneously. The final verse, with the references to sights flashing before one's face, and the sun going down, sounds rather funereal; is the speaker mourning their own death, or the death of the relationship? Either way, combined with the references to paradise and atonement, there's a somewhat purgatorial quality to the song, which we also find in "my tears ricochet" (*folklore*).

There are connections with "tolerate it" and "champagne problems," other songs on *evermore* with similar themes. The frequent rhetorical questions emphasize a speaker trying to figure out where it all went wrong—a common theme in Swift's music (for example in "How Did It End?" and "The Story of Us"). The inconsistent rhyme and ambiguous syntax suggest we are hearing a stream of consciousness from both speakers, as they muse on fragmented images and flashbacks from the relationship in question. The references to centerfolds and podium also imply a connection with the world of celebrity, and might reflect poignantly on Swift's own experience.

ivy

A fitting symbol for a love affair that quickly grows out of control, is impossible to shake off, and can be destructive

How's one to know?

Universality

I'd meet you where the spirit meets the bones

Graveyard, or an allusion to an album by Lucinda Williams or poem by Miller Williams

In a **f**aith **f**orgotten land

In from the snow

Metaphor for the marriage?

Your touch brought forth an incandescent glow

The affair offering warmth and light in a cold expanse

Tarnished but so grand

Sullied—antiquated language fits the "fountain pen" vibe of the song

And the old widow goes to the stone every day

But I don't, I just sit here and wait

Grieving for the living

Stuck in limbo, unable to mourn, yet feeling widowed already

Oh, goddamn

My **p**ain fits in the **p**alm of your freezing hand

The "freezing hand" perhaps implies how her lover has awoken her ability to feel again after being "forgotten"

Taking mine, but it's been promised to another

Oh, I can't

Stop you putting roots in my dreamland

My house of stone, your ivy grows

And now I'm covered in you

Implies an intense power of the affair, both sexually and outwardly—it could destroy everything

I wish to know

Alliteration as in "faith forgotten"

The **f**atal **f**law that makes you long to be

Magnificently cursed

Bittersweet, paradoxical fairy tale

He's in the room

Your opal eyes are all I wish to see

Allure and richness in the lover's eyes—opal is associated with love and eroticism

He wants what's only yours

chorus repeats

Clover blooms in the fields

Spring breaks loose, the time is near

What would he do if he found us out?

Crescent moon, coast is clear

Spring breaks loose, but so does fear

He's gonna burn this house to the ground

Imagery of blooming flowers and the moon allude to fertility and pregnancy; "Spring breaks loose" may euphemistically imply female arousal

The speaker as a house covered in ivy suggests not only that her husband will destroy the adulterous relationship, but may even destroy the speaker too

How's one to know?

I'd live and die for moments that we stole

On begged and borrowed time

So tell me to run *The speaker commands her lover to tell her what to do*

Or dare to sit and watch what we'll become

And drink my husband's wine

Becoming is a key theme, also in the lines that might allude to pregnancy

chorus repeats

So yeah, it's a fire

It's a goddamn blaze in the dark

And you started it

You started it

She blames her lover for the destruction of the marriage, but "so yeah" suggests it was inevitable, even welcome

So yeah, it's a war *See also "The Great War"*

It's the goddamn fight of my life

And you started it

You started it

chorus repeats

In you, you

Now I'm covered in you

In you *Ends on a fitting reference to the love object*

IVY

[analysis]

This song is full of rich imagery characteristic of the *folklore/evermore* era: green vines, fire, stone houses, blossom, the moon, opals. It has a mythological quality to it, and makes effective use of the contrast between dull, cold stone and bright, blazing fire to emphasize the transformative nature of a love affair. It's one of several songs on the two albums that focus on adultery, including "illicit affairs" and "no body no crime."

The central image is of ivy creeping over a stone house, alluding to something that grows slowly but has a profound effect, and there are also hints at the passionate, sexual nature of the affair in the language of blooming, the moon, and glowing. Love as something that covers a body and leaves physical marks is a very Swiftian trope, whether it's scars, wine stains, or, in this case, ivy.

The song uses multiple metaphors and symbols to describe the way in which one feels at the mercy of another when deeply in love: pain fitting into a hand, a house covered inexorably in creeping vines. We might recall the image of Swift entwined in viny tendrils in the "Out Of The Woods" video; here, this engulfment by plants is framed in a more positive and poetic light; the speaker longs to be *in* the woods, not out of them (see also "willow"). The song shows a tension between hesitant, fearful uncertainty (several rhetorical questions) and the speaker's resigned, determined acceptance of fate: "so yeah," "it's the goddamn fight of my life." The frequent second-person addresses to the object of the song imply intimacy but also fit with her assertion that "you started it": it's a song about the irrevocable chain of events that this lover has set in motion.

marjorie

Never be so kind, you forget to be clever

Never be so clever, you forget to be kind

Antimetabole prompts the listener to really reflect on what these two concepts mean in relation to each other

And if I didn't know better

Stream of consciousness

I'd think you were talking to me now

If I didn't know better

I'd think you were still around

What died didn't stay dead

What died didn't stay dead

You're alive, you're alive in my head

What died didn't stay dead

What died didn't stay dead

You're alive, so alive

The frequent repetition and juxtaposition in this song evoke a kind of haunting

Never be so polite, you forget your power

Never wield such power, you forget to be polite

"Wield" as an archaic association with weapons; the improper use of power is a violent act

And if I didn't know better

Contrast of tragic adult knowledge (Marjorie has passed) with the strong desire to hold onto a childlike fantasy

I'd think you were listening to me now

If I didn't know better

I'd think you were still around

The repetition with variation here is poignant—now Marjorie is listening to Swift, who has carried on her musical legacy

What died didn't stay dead

What died didn't stay dead

You're alive, you're alive in my head

"Head" and "dead" are some of the only perfect rhymes—Marjorie lives on in memory

What died didn't stay dead

What died didn't stay dead

You're alive, so alive

The autumn chill that wakes me up

We move to a series of Swiftian tableaux—the sense that we are admitted access to these flashbacks in real time

You loved the amber skies so much

Pathetic fallacy: in the autumn of Marjorie's life, the speaker remembers her as vivid and bright

Long limbs and frozen swims

You'd always go past where our feet could touch

Inaccessibility is particularly poignant, referring as it does to the fact that children might grow up to feel they never properly got to know their grandparents

And I complained the whole way there

The car ride back and up the stairs

I should've asked you questions

I should've asked you how to be

Anaphora puts the speaker's regret on display

Asked you to write it down for me

Should've kept every grocery store receipt

A very Swiftian image—the tangible leftover artifacts of lost love. The mundanity of the symbol makes it extra poignant

'Cause every scrap of you would be taken from me

Passive voice as powerlessness

Watched as you signed your name Marjorie

All your closets of backlogged dreams

Stage outfits and aspirations. The use of the closet suggests unfulfilled potential

And how you left them all to me

Actual inheritance—but also the way in which Swift's grandmother shaped her career

chorus repeats

And if I didn't know better

I'd think you were singing to me now

The song includes Marjorie's vocals in the background, bringing these lyrics to life

If I didn't know better

I'd think you were still around

I know better

But I still feel you all around

I know better

The shift to admitting she knows better, but Marjorie is still around, emphasizes the endurance of Marjorie's legacy

But you're still around

MARJORIE

[analysis]

This song fits into the genre of elegy, a poem or song that remembers the dead, and the genre dates back to classical antiquity. "marjorie" is written in honor of Marjorie Finlay, Swift's opera singer grandmother, who passed away in Swift's early teens and whose influence played a role in Taylor's pursuit of a career in music (Swift's song "Timeless" is also dedicated to her). The song combines a series of simple yet resonant images with devices such as repetition and antimetabole to evoke the speaker's vivid flashbacks, the way Marjorie lives on in her memory, and the realization of the values her grandmother taught her. The use of second-person address and sentences beginning with "and" give the feeling that we are listening to a spontaneous monologue delivered by the speaker. This plays slightly with the genre of elegy, which is traditionally more formal.

Even though childhood is not explicitly mentioned in the song, there's a clear sense of the speaker's formative years and Marjorie's influence, accompanied by the universal tragedy of a child never fully getting to know his or her grandparent; the autumnal imagery serves to emphasize this, evocative of the way in which we meet our grandparents during the autumn of their lives. A juxtaposition runs through the song, between Marjorie's being just out of reach and yet forever omnipresent. As in so many Swift songs, everyday objects become invested with a wealth of emotion, here symbolizing the meaning retrospectively attributed to "every scrap" of a person by mourners in the wake of their death.

The shift in the chorus, from "talking," to "listening," to "singing," subtly suggests a poignant progression: from Swift's taking advice from Marjorie, to forging her own path and career with Marjorie as listener and spectator, to eventual collaboration: Marjorie's vocals can be heard in the background of the song alongside Swift's, forming a harmony between the two singers that reflects the way Marjorie is still "all around."

chapter ten

MIDNIGHTS

Maroon

As if we are overhearing a conversation

When the morning came we were cleaning incense off your vinyl shelf

'Cause we lost track of time again

Laughing with my feet in your **l**ap

Like you were my closest friend

Reported speech

"How'd we end up on the floor anyway?" You **s**ay

"Your roommate'**s** cheap-a**ss** **s**crew-top ros**é**, that's how"

Four trochees in a row. A rhythmic effect, almost the aural equivalent of an underline

I **s**ee you every day now

Shifts in tense—past, present, and back to past—seem to haunt the speaker

And I chose you

Double rhyme lends intimacy. In choosing "you," she is vulnerable and uninhibited ("no shoes")

The one I was dancin' with

In New York, no shoes

Looked up at the sky and it was

Enjambment indicates the sky was burgundy in color, but there is a disjointedness here

The burgundy on my T-shirt when you splashed your wine into me

Collision

And how the blood rushed into my cheeks, so scarlet, it was

A rush of memories

The mark you saw on my collarbone, the rust that grew between telephones

The relationship is over

Tricolon The lips I used to call home, so scarlet, it was maroon

A progression from light to dark

The growth of rust to indicate a lack of communication amplifies its emotional burden

When the silence came, **w**e **w**ere shaking blind and hazy

Personified

How the **h**ell did we lose sight of us again?

Sobbin' with your **h**ead in your **h**ands

Vivid tableaux

Ain't that the way shit always ends?

Moves from wistful recollection to anger

You were standin' **h**ollow-eyed in the **h**allway

Carnations you had thought were roses, that's us

I feel you no matter what

Misunderstanding as a core element of the relationship

The rubies that I gave up *Suggests the object of the song is (red or maroon) rubies*

And I lost you *The movement from "chose" to "lost" tells a whole story in a single song*

The one I was dancin' with

In New York, no shoes

Looked up at the sky and it was maroon

The burgundy on my T-shirt when you splashed your wine into me

And how the blood rushed into my cheeks, so scarlet, it was (maroon)

The mark you saw on my collarbone, the rust that grew between telephones

The lips I used to call home, so scarlet, it was (maroon)

And I wake with your **mem**ory over **me**

That's a real fucking legacy, legacy (it was maroon)

The object still haunts her

And I wake with your memory over me

That's a real fucking legacy to leave

The syntax is ambiguous here: the legacy that the object left, or was (the act of) leaving the legacy?

Profanity renders the legacy ironic

The burgundy on my T-shirt when you splashed your wine into me

And how the blood rushed into my cheeks, so scarlet (it was maroon)

The mark you saw on my collarbone, the rust that grew between telephones

The lips I used to call home, so scarlet (it was maroon)

Echoes "exile": a relationship as a familiar place from which one can become an exile or foreigner

It was maroon

It was maroon

Enigmatic, unsatisfying conclusion

"Maroon" harks back to Red. Darker still than the blood, rubies, and scarlet mentioned in the song, it may signify the way memories of a relationship mature and change with time

MAROON

[analysis]

“Maroon,” a song that seems to refer back to Swift’s album *Red* and its title track, reflects on a past relationship whose complicated legacy still haunts the speaker. The switch between past and present tense occurs frequently as the speaker recalls the love affair in flashbacks and images that seem to appear spontaneously to her in quick succession, while musing on its continued presence in *her* present. The lack of a regular rhyme scheme (there’s frequent double rhyme, slant rhyme and no rhyme), combined with the ambiguous grammar (anacoluthon) and often incomplete sentences, adds to the feeling that we are tapping into a stream of consciousness from the speaker’s mind, but also overhearing her tell us a story. She uses concise, vivid images that hold a wealth of meaning to mirror the way in which memories and images of past relationships appear to us, often unbidden, in times of emotional reflection. A particularly interesting aspect of the song is the way in which absence becomes presence: a lack of communication grows like rust; silence *arrives*; a long-gone lover leaves an ever-present legacy. This reflects the way in which loss—heartbreak or bereavement—often feels like a physical pain or burden.

There is quite a lot of alliteration, particularly sibilance, which lends a softness to the song that contrasts sharply with the use of profanity in its later parts: as with many Swift songs, the speaker undergoes a journey from wistful reminiscence to angry reflection. The symbolism of maroon has many possible interpretations, but certainly seems to suggest a progression of sorts from the red of "Red" and *Red*, and of blood and scarlet: there's a sense of time passing, of something darkening (blood drying?), and growing more mature. This is also nicely reflected in the move from rosé to burgundy in the imagery of the wine.

You're On Your Own, Kid

Summer went away *Pathetic fallacy*

Still, the yearning stays *Pleasing symmetry of bookended alliteration*

I play it cool with the best of them

I wait patiently

He's gonna notice me

It's okay, we're the best of friends

Anyway *"It's okay" and "anyway" are conversational, but read as if she is lying to herself*

I hear it in your voice *Shift from third person to direct address often coincides with a change in tone*

You're smoking with your boys

I touch my phone as if it's your face *Remarkably conveys the poignant loneliness of the speaker*

I didn't choose this town

I dream of getting out

There's just one who could make me stay

All my days

From sprinkler splashes to fireplace ashes *Circularity, both in the cycle of the year and the speaker's waiting. From childlike happiness to spent fire with no warmth left*

I waited ages to see you there

I search the party of better bodies *Microcosm of insecurity*

Just to learn that you never cared

You're on your own, kid *Speaking to herself, suggesting she feels an enduring alienation or sense of betrayal*

You always have been

I see the great escape

So long, Daisy May *Perhaps a farewell to her younger self, and sets up the next line*

I picked the petals, he loves me not

Something different bloomed

A shift in the floral metaphor: she channels her energy into songwriting instead of a boy

Writing in my room

I play my songs in the parking lot

Suggests stasis, contrasted with the speaker's dream of running away

I'll run away

From sprinkler splashes to fireplace ashes

I called a taxi to take me there

I search the party of better bodies

Just to learn that my dreams aren't rare

Difficulty of standing out in the music industry

You're on your own, kid

You always have been

From sprinkler splashes to fireplace ashes

I gave my blood, sweat, and tears for this

Remarkably conveys the poignant loneliness of the speaker

I hosted parties and starved my body

Swift references disordered eating in *Miss Americana*

Like I'd be saved by a perfect kiss

Disillusionment that comes when fantasy fails to match up with reality

The jokes weren't funny, I took the money

Internal rhyme suggests her strategy for dealing with mockery was to profit, or in a more sinister context, that she was silenced

My friends from home don't know what to say

I looked around in a blood-soaked gown

Recalls the horror film *Carrie*. It suggests gaining strength from adversity and using it to fortify oneself against one's enemies. It also suggests paying a terrible price for that power

And I saw something they can't take away

Integrity

'Cause there were pages turned with the bridges burned

Every conflict a progression

Everything you lose is a step you take

So make the friendship bracelets

Take the moment and taste it

You've got no reason to be afraid

Encapsulates fans' feelings that Swift is an empathetic best friend and counselor of sorts

. . . Yeah, you can face this . . .

YOU'RE ON YOUR OWN, KID

[analysis]

"You're On Your Own, Kid," or "YOYOK," is one of Swift's most beloved songs, although relatively recent in her catalogue. It's very difficult *not* to read this song autobiographically, as so many of its references seem to overlap almost exactly with what we know about Swift herself, and her career path. Despite this, YOYOK has gained status as perhaps one of the most relatable songs of Swift's oeuvre. A tweet by Swiftie lyric analyst @tweetsricochet, "I've said it before and I'll say it again, you can tell exactly what sort of person you are from the lyric you most relate to in YOYOK," received over 600 comments and 2,000 retweets. That the central refrain resonates so strongly with Swift's fans is perhaps unsurprising: who among us has *not* felt misunderstood, different, and alone, at least once in our lives, and constructed a narrative wherein we've always been that way? It's clear why this is track 5 on *Midnights*: its central refrain is quietly heartbreaking.

This song has quite short lines compared to many of Swift's others. Fitting with this, its language and images are spare, but imbued with a wealth of meaning: the extended metaphor of the daisy is a good example, shifting with significance in every line. The semantics of wistful summer are startlingly contrasted with those of blood, sweat and tears, emphasizing the rocky road of the speaker's "great escape" and the finding of empowerment in pain. It's a reminder that Swift offers in her other songs, too: we are the sum of our trials and tribulations, and every painful moment in youth makes us the adult we become. This is emphasized by moments of internal rhyme, culminating in the comforting assertion that we're doing just fine.

The song illustrates the beauty of brevity, and Swift's ability to evoke deep sensations with the simplest phrase or image. The friendship bracelets are an excellent example: this throwaway line launched a lasting trend and tangible gesture of solidarity among fans, reminding us that, in fact, *none* of us is ever really on our own, kid.

The Great War

A name often used for the First World War

My knuckles were bruised like violets *Jarring simile*

Sucker punching walls, cursed you as I sleep-talked *Futile rage*

Spineless in my tomb of silence *Internal slant rhyme—self-destructive*

Tore your banners down, took the battle underground *"Would've, Could've, Should've"*

And maybe it was ego swinging

Maybe it was her

Flashes *Analepsis* of the **b**attle come back to me in a **b**lur

All that bloodshed, **c**rimson **c**lover *Gruesome image of bloodstained ground* *Emotional pain*

Uh-huh, sweet dream was over

My hand was the one you reached for

All throughout the Great War *Swift uses the First World War as a relationship metaphor. See also Sylvia Plath's unsettling poem, "Daddy"*

Always remember *Imperative*

Uh-huh, tears on the letter *Heartbreak, but alludes to the letters exchanged in the actual "Great War"*

I vowed not to cry anymore

If we survived the Great War

You drew up some good faith treaties *Diplomacy*

I drew curtains closed, drank my poison all alone *Self-destructive behavior. Possible allusion to Hitler's wife's suicide in the Second World War*

You said I have to trust more freely

But **d**iesel is **d**esire, you were playin' with fire *The lover set fire to the fuel of her desire*

And maybe it's the past that's talkin'

Screamin' from the crypt *Intangible notion of the past given a voice*

Tellin' me to punish you for things you never did

So I justified it

All that bloodshed, crimson clover

Uh-huh, the bombs were close and *Swift returns to the imagery of bombs in TTPD where she plays on the meaning of "love bombing"*

My hand was the one you reached for

All throughout the Great War

Always remember

Uh-huh, the burning embers

The flames are dying down as the song progresses—a journey from self-destructive violence to reconciliation

I vowed not to fight anymore

If we survived the Great War

It turned into something bigger

After an explosion or "Lavender Haze" of falling in love

Somewhere in the haze, got a sense I'd been betrayed

Slant rhyme of haze/betrayed suggests that the speaker's addled senses are making her believe things that aren't true

Your finger on my hair pin triggers

Soldier down on that icy ground

Looked up at me with honor and truth

Broken and **b**lue, so I called off the troops

Speaker is quick to anger/easily triggered. The hairpin link to "right where you left me" potentially suggests a queer reading

Plosive sounds mirror the idea of bombs

That was the night I nearly lost you

I really thought I lost you

Repetition as she realizes impact of her behavior

We can plant a memory garden

Say a solemn prayer, place a poppy in my hair

Poppy is a symbol of the First World War and trench warfare in Europe. This reference is a bit unsettling

There's no morning glory, it was war, it wasn't fair

And we will never go back

Regeneration: morning glories bloom each morning. The damage of those "war" years cannot be undone (hence the memory garden)

To that bloodshed, crimson clover

Uh-huh, the worst was over

My hand was the one you reached for

All throughout the Great War

Always remember

Uh-huh, we're **b**urned for **b**etter

I vowed I would always be yours

The two lovers have undergone a trial by fire that has strengthened their relationship

'Cause we survived the Great War

I would always be yours

'Cause we survived the Great War

I vowed I would always be yours

Vow mirrors the "solemn prayer"

THE GREAT WAR

[analysis]

Swift often uses the metaphor of love as a war, which dates back to classical antiquity and was particularly popular in Renaissance sonnets by poets such as Francis Petrarch, Philip Sidney, John Donne, and Thomas Wyatt. However, this is perhaps her fullest exploration of it. She invokes imagery from both the First and Second World Wars (and potentially earlier—the reference to banners evokes warfare in the Middle Ages) to frame a difficult relationship in terms of a series of battles. She uses unsettling juxtapositions—knuckles bruised like violets, crimson clover—to create a sense of unease that perhaps mirrors the unease in a new relationship that is the subject of the song. "Great war" is, in itself, a rather awkward paradox, since there is nothing great (in its modern sense of "good") about war, but rather the term "great" might refer to the magnitude and duration of the conflict, which also fits the metaphor—the struggles felt enormous to the speaker at the time.

The song alludes to self-destructive behavior that

is framed in terms of violence, and echoes some of the imagery in “Would’ve, Could’ve, Should’ve”—except in that song, the speaker is the victim of the violence rather than its instigator. This song seems to describe a period of growth, in which the speaker learns to “trust more freely” and overcome her emotional baggage (personified as the past screaming from the crypt). She atones for the injuries and harm she has inflicted on her lover (a similar sentiment to that voiced in “Afterglow”), contrasting his “honor and truth” with her spineless silence. His ice can cool the fire of her self-destructive tendencies, leaving only a branded scar (“burned for better”) that serves as a reminder never to unleash that pain again. There is a key opposition running throughout the poem between delicate flowers and harsh violence, which might hint at the fact that, just as with the poppies on Flanders fields, something beautiful can grow out of sorrow and chaos.

Bigger Than The Whole Sky

A lack or absence, foreshadows what is to come

No words appear before me in the aftermath *Negative connotation of disaster*

Salt streams out my eyes and into my ears

Every single thing I touch becomes sick with sadness

'Cause it's all over now, all out to sea

Sibilance reflects the trickling tears in an image of the speaker lying on her back. Sadness touches all her senses, which anticipates the next line

Somatic

Idiom echoes the watery language and sense of loss and feeling adrift

Goodbye, goodbye, goodbye

You were bigger than the whole sky *Hyperbole stresses the extreme emotions*

You were more than just a short time

And I've got a lot to pine about

I've got a lot to live without

Tricolon and direct address to the object of the song

Anaphora emphasizes the struggle to describe something that ended before it reached its full potential

I'm never gonna meet

What could've been, would've been

What should've been you

What could've been, would've been you

Intriguing and ambiguous word to use, suggesting the song is not about the end of an established relationship (of whatever kind), but one that never even began

Allusion to "the butterfly effect"

Did some bird flap its wings over in Asia? *A nice (likely coincidental) connection to Charlotte Smith's poem "The Swallow"*

Did some force take you because I didn't pray?

Every single thing to come has turned into ashes

'Cause it's all over, it's not meant to be

So I'll say words I don't believe

Anaphora of rhetorical questions. Looking to higher external forces for an explanation

Recurring metaphor in Midnights. Anticipates exhaustion from "rising from the ashes" in "You're Losing Me"

Goodbye, goodbye, goodbye

You were bigger than the whole sky

You were more than just a short time

And I've got a lot to pine about

I've got a lot to live without

I'm never gonna meet

What could've been, would've been

What should've been you

The chorus cycles through multiple tenses: past, present, future, then conditional, to express the impact of the loss

What could've been, would've been

What should've been you

(What could've been, would've been)

What could've been, would've been you

(Could've been, would've been)

(Could've been, would've been)

Multiple repeated conditional phrases stress that this song is rooted in the hypothetical: potential that never came to fruition

Goodbye, goodbye, goodbye

You were bigger than the whole sky

You were more than just a short time

And I've got a lot to pine about

I've got a lot to live without

I'm never gonna meet

What could've been, would've been

What should've been you

"So I'll say words I don't believe" puts the listener in an awkward position with a now unreliable narrator: how are we supposed to interpret the words, then? Alternatively, it could suggest the speaker's unsteady faith, but that she'll try anything—even prayer—to fix the situation. See also: "Holy orange bottles, each night I pray to you / Desperate people find faith, so now I pray to Jesus too" from "Soon You'll Get Better"

BIGGER THAN THE WHOLE SKY

[analysis]

This song reads like an elegy: a lament for one who has died. It shares certain parallels in imagery with "You're Losing Me," which might also be interpreted as an elegy, but for the speaker herself. "Bigger Than The Whole Sky" is often discussed by fans as a cathartic song that has helped them process various types of grief, particularly miscarriage and baby loss, and this is probably owing to its vagueness. The mourning of lost potential, speculating painfully about what might have been but never will be, is applicable to so many situations, and thus is characteristic of Swift's highly relatable lyrics. The frequent repetition of conditional phrases roots the song in the hypothetical but impossible, as the speaker grieves lost potential. The repeated "goodbye" and frequent rhetorical questions suggest a speaker trying to process what has happened in the "aftermath" of loss, using somatic (bodily) imagery to highlight the ways in which the loss is so deep that it feels physical. The fact that the speaker must be lying on her back for tears to stream into her ears evokes a poignant parallel with "Lavender Haze," which begins, "'staring at the ceiling with you." Here, however, the staring is one of apathetic despair rather than companionable calm.

There is a somewhat meta aspect to the song: the speaker admits, while singing, that she is saying words she does not believe. This frames her as a somewhat unreliable narrator, not for the first time in Swift's oeuvre. It points to our tendency to mask vulnerable feelings for our audience, something Swift explores in many of her lyrics (see, for example, "The Very First Night" and "I Can Do It With a Broken Heart"). Alternatively, the line might be read as referring to prayers the speaker doesn't entirely believe in, showcasing her desperation—something we also find in "Soon You'll Get Better" on *Lover*. This ambiguity again perhaps accounts for the flexibility and versatility of the song as an elegy among Swift's fans.

Hits Different

I washed my hands of us at the club

You **m**ade a **m**ess of me *An exploration of the mess a broken heart can make of us, emotionally and physically*

I pictured you with other girls in love

Then threw up on the street *A bathetic and decidedly unromantic surprise*

Like waiting for a bus that never shows *A blend of hope and impatience that eventually ends in resignation*

You just start walkin' on *Second-person address*

They say that if it's right, you know

Each bar plays our song

Nothing has ever felt so wrong *Anacoluthon. Left alone, "they say if it's right, you know / each bar plays our song" is pleasantly serendipitous. Instead, "nothing has ever felt so wrong" ties this up as ominous—a doomed relationship*

Oh my, love is a lie *Neat internal rhyme*

Shit my friends say to get me by *Anacoluthon, and ambiguous: her friends try and console her by telling her love doesn't really exist; OR, her friends are telling her nonsense to try and cheer her up*

It hits different *Swiftian pun on physical blows as emotional pain*

It hits different this time

Catastrophic blues *Hyperbole* *Associated with a paricular lover in Swift's discography*

Movin' on was always easy for me to do

It hits different

It hits different 'cause it's you

('Cause it's you) *Big reveal—this relationship was like no other (See: "Daylight")*

I used to switch out these Kens, I'd just ghost *Implies other lovers were replaceable* *Anticipates "My Boy Only Breaks His Favorite Toys"*

Rip the Band-Aid off and skip town like an asshole outlaw *Evokes "cowboy like me"* *Idiom for doing something painful quickly for the sake of healing*

Freedom felt like summer then on the coast

Now the sun burns my heart and the sand hurts my feelings *Echoes "I realized freedom ain't nothing but missing you" from "Back To December"*

And I never don't cry (no, I never don't cry) at the bar *Double negative*

Yeah, my sadness is contagious (my sadness is contagious)

I slur your name 'til someone puts me in a car

Either physically had to put her in the car due to her drunken state, or she's lost all interest in what happens to her

I stopped receiving invitations

Ambiguous isolation—the invitations ceased or did she cut herself off from others?

chorus repeats

Sacred relics, as in "I Can Do It With a Broken Heart"

I find the artifacts, cried over a hat

Cursed the space that I needed

Deliberate bathos that is both amusing and deeply sad

The speaker doesn't really want to move on

I trace the evidence, **m**ake it **m**ake some sense

Anticipates "How Did It End?"

Internal rhyme of "evidence" and "sense" explores the speaker's desperate need to find logic and closure

Why the wound is still bleedin'

You were the one that I loved

Past tense is poignant

Don't need another metaphor, it's simple enough

Meta, but also ironic

A wrinkle in time like the crease by your eyes

Allusion to the novel by Madeleine L'Engle about traveling through space and time. A long-term relationship has passed in the blink of an eye. The crease by his eyes (part of his smile) had the metaphorical ability to transport her into other worlds

This is why they shouldn't kill off the main guy

Dreams of your hair and your stare and sense of belief

In the good in the world, you once believed in me

Enjambment delivers the surprise: he believes in the good in the world, but not in her anymore

And I felt you and I held you for a while

Bet I could still melt your world

Defiance

Argumentative, antithetical dream girl

Mocking the "manic pixie dream girl" film trope. She's decidedly not passive or ethereal for the benefit of the "main guy" above; rather, she's paradoxical and argumentative in a way he may have found alluring

I heard your key turn in the door down the hallway

Is that your key in the door?

Is it okay? Is it you?

Or have they come to take me away?

To take me away

Evokes a troubling history of women who were taken away for, among other things, having strong emotions

Strong parallels with the final scene of Tennessee Williams's A Streetcar Named Desire, where Blanche DuBois believes, in her catatonic state, that an old flame is coming to help her

chorus repeats

HITS DIFFERENT

[analysis]

If "Blank Space" was where Swift first decided to satirize the "crazy ex-girlfriend" trope by really leaning into it, "Hits Different" continues in the same vein—but this time she's the "crazy *heartbroken* ex," whose behavior has become so unhinged that it unnerves polite society. There's something particularly unsettling about the line "have they come to take me away?," which reflects a very real history of women who didn't fit social norms being locked up in asylums to prevent them becoming an inconvenience to (usually) men. Famous fictional examples include Blanche DuBois from Tennessee Williams's *A Streetcar Named Desire* and Bertha Mason from Charlotte Brontë's *Jane Eyre,* but it happened frequently in real life, too. The final (official) song on *Midnights,* "Hits Different" ends with the possibility of the speaker's being institutionalized. *The Tortured Poets Department* seems to follow directly from this—"I was supposed to be sent away, but they forgot to come and get me"—a fan theory that Swift seemingly confirmed by liking it on social media. Like “mad woman,” “Hits Different” is potentially a nod to the ways in which bad male behavior can induce in women strong emotions that the patriarchy then gaslights them into believing are symptoms of psychological illness.

The song is rich in bodily imagery—vomiting, ugly crying, bleeding, disease, burning—exploring the fine line between being broken-hearted and losing one’s grip on reality. It’s full of hyperbole to reflect the extreme feelings that surface during grief, and anacoluthon to express the way in which the speaker flits wildly from one thought or notion to another, reflective of someone not quite in her right mind. Ironically for a song that declares it doesn’t need any more metaphors, it’s also rich in metaphors, as the speaker tries to find the right words to articulate her turbulent feelings.

You're Losing Me (*From the Vault*)

"You're Losing Me" begins gently and sadly, backtracked by the sound of a heartbeat (something Swift also does in "Wildest Dreams," albeit with a rather more upbeat tempo). It immediately plunges the speaker into the middle of a breakdown in communication between two lovers.

Two negatives set the tone

You say, "I don't understand, " and I say, "I know you don't" *In media res*

We thought a cure would come through in time, now I fear it won't

Imperative, question, or recollection?

Remember lookin' at this room, we loved it 'cause of the light *Recalls the relationship in "Daylight"*

Now, I just sit in the dark and wonder if it's time

Arc of the relationship from light to dark

Do I throw out everything we built or keep it?

I'm getting tired even for a phoenix *Assonance helps express that she gave him everything she had*

Always risin' from the ashes

Mendin' all her gashes

You might just have dealt the final blow *Swift writes of her ability to bounce back in "Labyrinth," "Look What You Made Me Do," "willow," and "Hits Different," making these lines poignant and final*

Stop, you're losin' me

Stop, you're losin' me

Stop, you're losin' me

I can't find a pulse

My heart won't start anymore *"Losing me" as a literal death. "Anymore" signifies a pattern, but they have always managed to restart it—until now*

For you *She is not dying, but rather her love for him*

'Cause you're losin' me

The grammar and syntax of the song are particularly interesting: there are multiple occasions where a new line changes our understanding of the previous line. This technique keeps the listener in suspense, wondering how the story is going to progress, and alert to unexpected surprises. This perhaps mirrors the feelings of the speaker herself, waiting on edge, torn between her desire to "throw out everything we built or keep it." The song is fairly light on rhyme, sounding more like a conversation or monologue, or even a eulogy for a deceased love affair.

Symbol of renewal in Swift's lyrics—a need for decisive action to break this stalemate

Every mornin', I glared at you with storms in my eyes

How can you say that you love someone you can't tell is dyin'?

I sent you signals and bit my nails down to the quick *To the core*

My face was gray, but you wouldn't admit that we were sick *The relationship as diseased*

Anticipates "getting color back into my face" in "So Long, London"

And the air is thick with loss and indecision

A lack of something has a tangible, physical presence

I know my pain is such an imposition

Now, you're runnin' down the hallway

"Hollow-eyed in the hallway" from "Maroon"

And you know what they all say

You don't know what you got until it's gone

chorus repeats

How long could we be a sad song *Swiftian trope*

Anticipates "I stopped CPR after all it's no use" in "So Long, London"

'Til we were too far gone to bring back to life?

I gave you all my best me's, my endless empathy

Assonance helps express that she gave him everything she had

And all I did was bleed as I tried to be the bravest soldier

Role reversal from "The Great War"

Fighting in only your army *Total devotion*

Frontlines, don't you ignore me

I'm the best thing at this party *Shift from devotion to indignation*

(You're losin' me)

The song paints a picture of happier times before fading into imagery of sickness, darkness, and pain, then climaxes in the tragic crescendo of the bridge, in which the speaker voices her grief, anger, and desperation for the object of the song to act. This tension, between urging him to stop and begging him to start, characterizes the whole song, which is rich in imperatives that emphasize the speaker's pleas.

And I wouldn't marry me either *Change in syntax (third person) toward harsh self-reflection and despair*

A **p**athological **p**eople **p**leaser *Pathology fits with the song's imagery of bodies and death—a nearly medical examination of negative traits*

Who only wanted you to see her

And I'm fadin', thinkin' *Implies a slow death ("gray face"). The music here does not fade but instead rises to a crescendo*

"Do something, babe, say something" (say something)

"Lose something, babe, risk something" (you're losin' me) *Epistrophe*

"Choose something, babe, I got nothing (got nothing) *Contrast in "something" and "nothing"—his stasis has reduced her to nothingness*

To believe *Enjambment reveals a twist. "I got nothing" works alone, but specifically, she has lost faith*

Unless you're choosin' me"

Ultimatum

Swift has often used the imagery of a broken, dying, or sick body to describe a relationship in difficulty, but here it takes the shape of an extended metaphor that permeates the entire song. For a song that frames the speaker as dying, the bridge is surprisingly passionate, sounding almost like a desperate last gasp (the "death rattle breathing," perhaps, as she'd later say in "How Did It End?").

You're losin' me

Stop (stop, stop), you're losin' me

Stop (stop, stop), you're losin' me

Pleading "stop" (like her heart), but also asking the object to "do something." The object appears to be doing all the wrong things but none of the right things

I can't find a pulse

My heart won't start anymore

Fittingly final

chapter eleven

THE TORTURED POETS DEPARTMENT

So Long, London

I saw in **m**y **m**ind fairy lights through the **m**ist
I **k**ept **c**alm and **c**arried the weight of the rift
Pulled him in **t**ighter each **t**ime he was drifting away
My **s**pine **s**plit from carrying us up the hill
Wet through my clothes, **w**eary bones caught the chill
I stopped trying to make him laugh
Stopped trying to drill the safe
Thinkin', how much sad did you think I had
Did you think I had in me?
Oh, the tragedy …

So long, London
You'll find someone …

I didn't opt in to be your odd man out
I founded the club she's heard great things about
I left all I knew, you left me at the **h**ouse by the **H**eath
I stopped CPR, after all it's no use
The spirit was gone, we would never come to
And I'm pissed off you let me give you all that youth for free

For so long, London
Stitches undone
Two **g**raves, one **g**un
I'll find someone …
And you say I abandoned the ship

London is known as the "Big Smoke" and is associated with fog. It may also be a confusion or haze in the speaker's memories

Evokes "Lover"

A rift is crack or gap, and technically weightless. The absence of something can feel, paradoxically, like a burden

A play on a British saying to put on a brave face

Pauses on "drift" to rhyme with "rift" before continuing to "-ing away." It's the opposite of enjambment, reflecting the stop-start nature of the relationship

Image recurs in "The Black Dog"

Alludes to the Greek myth of Sisyphus and his futile burden

The album often references a lover whose "blues" render him cold

Stops (caesura) on "drill"

Internal rhyme and backtracking, as if the speaker is wrestling with the decision

Apostrophe maximizes the gravitas. Tragedy is also referenced in "The Black Dog"

Metonymy—the place associated with a person to represent that person in the lyrics

The repetition makes the contrast more jarring

Assonance of the "ou" sound gives the line a slightly echoing quality (like the choir vocals)

Presumably a reference to Hampstead Heath, London

Echoes "You're Losing Me"

Regain consciousness

Profanity in an otherwise poetic line suggests a barely suppressed rage

More broken/dying body imagery suggests they have tried to patch up this relationship before

A twist from the original use of "so long" (to mean goodbye) becomes its literal meaning—a long time

Deeply ambiguous. Perhaps both are "dying" in the space of the relationship, but only one of them actually ended it

Shipwrecks recur in TTPD—foundering relationship

Spontaneous monologue

But I was going down with it

My white knuckle dying grip

Assonance in these lines emphasizes "I," which is fitting as she voices her perspective

Holding tight to your quiet resentment and

My friends said it isn't right to be scared

Enjambment

Every day of a love affair

Every breath feels like rarest air

Anaphora of "every" here emphasizes that this pain had become routine

When you're not sure if he wants to be there

So how much sad did you think I had,

Did you think I had in me?

How much tragedy?

Just how low did you think I'd go?

Before I'd self-implode

Before I'd have to go be free

Self-imploding is a much sadder idea here than exploding, implying that she has turned all her pain inward and it will crush her silently

Assonance and repetition: wavering between hesitation and determination

You swore that you loved me but where were the clues?

I died on the altar waiting for the proof

Double significance: sacrificed on an altar, but also at the altar for marriage

You sacrificed us to the gods of your bluest days

And I'm just getting color back into my face

Implication is that his "blues" have drained her of color

I'm just mad as hell cause I loved this place

Ambiguous: her place in the relationship (like "the spot next to you" in "happiness") or London personified as the lover ("London Boy")

For so long, London

Had a good run

A moment of warm sun

Contrasts with descriptions of mist and "bluest days," above—they shared a warm moment but it has now faded. Possible link to the lover as the color gold, as in "invisible string" and "Daylight"

But I'm not the one

So long, London

Stitches undone

Two graves, one gun

You'll find someone . . .

Uncertainty

SO LONG, LONDON

[analysis]

Track 5 on *The Tortured Poets Department*, "So Long, London" is based on metonymy. "London" here stands not just for a place, but a long-term lover associated with that place (her "London Boy"), whom the speaker eventually had to leave—though not without regret. Like "How Did It End?," its sister track 5 on *The Anthology*, this song carries out a "postmortem" of a relationship, considering culpability and causality. The speaker is wistful and sad but also bitter and angry—clear in her moments of profanity—and takes pains to justify her actions and how hard she tried to "drill the safe" of her closed-off lover. "You say I abandoned the ship" is preemptively defensive, as if anticipating the other side of the story; we get the feeling we are overhearing a conversation here, but only one side of it.

Frequent repetition, alliteration, and assonance give the song a circular quality that perhaps also hints at the repetitiveness of the speaker trying to save the relationship while feeling scared and suffocated every day. The unusual use of caesura halts several lines just before the end, reflecting the speaker's hesitation as she had to decide whether to leave or not. The conversational use of "and" at the beginning of lines, along with rhetorical questions, give us the feeling we are hearing a spontaneous monologue, as the speaker asks both her (ex) lover, herself, and even us, her listeners, whether we really thought she could carry on like this forever.

Swift uses two of her most common tropes here: the metaphor of a relationship as a (dying or wounded) human body, and a relationship expressed in terms of the language of religion. "So Long, London" evokes a eulogy, a funeral reading for a relationship that died a slow, tortuous death. This feeling is amplified by the choral-style opening to the song.

loml

This poetic song is characteristic of *The Tortured Poets Department* in drawing from the semantic fields of forgery and religion. As in "The Smallest Man Who Ever Lived," the speaker would have died for the sins of the object of the song, but he tricked her with a facade and then sabotaged everything.

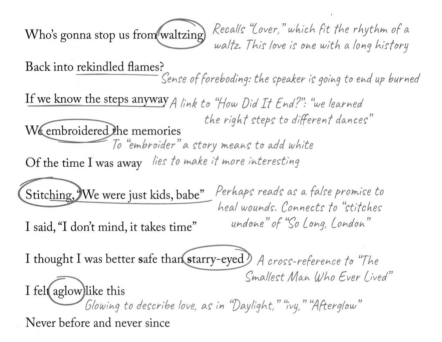

Who's gonna stop us from waltzing
Back into rekindled flames?
If we know the steps anyway
We embroidered the memories
Of the time I was away
Stitching, "We were just kids, babe"
I said, "I don't mind, it takes time"
I thought I was better safe than starry-eyed
I felt aglow like this
Never before and never since

Recalls "Lover," which fit the rhythm of a waltz. This love is one with a long history

Sense of foreboding: the speaker is going to end up burned

A link to "How Did It End?": "we learned the right steps to different dances"

To "embroider" a story means to add white lies to make it more interesting

Perhaps reads as a false promise to heal wounds. Connects to "stitches undone" of "So Long, London"

A cross-reference to "The Smallest Man Who Ever Lived"

Glowing to describe love, as in "Daylight," "ivy," "Afterglow"

By decoding the language of the song, we see that the relationship it describes was doomed from the beginning, wrapped up in "embroidery," forgery, and fakery by the "con man" who took the speaker for a fool. The rhetorical questions allude to the fact that the speaker may have known this, deep down, but was too "starry-eyed" to stop herself. The

beginning of the chorus on the conditional "if" also reflects the mood of the relationship: one of uncertainty and instability, with the promises turning out to be hollow.

If you know it in one glimpse, it's legendary

Second-person address adds intimacy

You and I go from one kiss to gettin' married

Still alive, killing time at the cemetery

Never quite buried

Funereal, but echoes the "Jehovah's Witness suit" of "The Smallest Man Who Ever Lived." He was presenting a facade

In your suit and tie, in the nick of time

Harks back to "killing time"

You lowdown boy, you stand up guy

Holy Ghost, you told me I'm

There is a pause between "I" and "m," as if to say she hangs on his every word

The love of your life

Love as religion. A pun that he will ghost her, but prior to that he seemed almost divine

You said I'm the love of your life

About a million times

Suggests this declaration was not quite sincere

Who's gonna tell me the truth

No one. TTPD is deeply concerned with truth and lies, and the nature of truth as potentially subjective

When you blew in with the winds of fate

Destiny and inevitability appear in "The Prophecy" and "But Daddy I Love Him"

And told me I reformed you

"I Can Fix Him (No Really I Can)"

When your impressionist paintings of Heaven

Turned out to be fakes

Echoes the references to colors in "illicit affairs" and "tolerate it," both of which frame an unequal relationship in terms of painting

Well, you took me to hell, too

Was was already there, and dragged her down with him?

In the reference to ink bleeding, Swift encapsulates wider concerns in *The Tortured Poets Department* with self-harm, writing as a form of catharsis, and, eventually, healing: the ink bleeds so that she doesn't have to. This song also echoes the prologue's reference to ticking love bombs, suggesting that the object of the song's exaggerated confessions of love turned out to be "dynamite" that destroyed her dreams.

And all at once, the ink bleeds *The prologue to TTPD refers to veins of black ink.*

A con man sells a fool a get-love-quick scheme *A love that looked good on paper is falling apart, but also writing as catharsis*

But I felt a hole like this *A reference to the Reputation poem, "Why She Disappeared"*

Never before, and ever since

Subtle shift from "never." Poignant revelation of the speaker's ongoing sadness

If you know it in one glimpse

It's legendary

What we thought was for all time

Was momentary

Still alive, killing time at the cemetery

An on-off relationship that they're waiting to funeralize

Never quite buried

Highlighting his role in this scripted, fake narrative

You cinephile in black and white *Contrast to the "impressionist paintings;" the reality is black and white. It also implies a draining of color associated with sadness*

All those plot twists and dynamite

Mr. Steal Your Girl, then make her cry *Alludes to the "tick, tick, tick of love bombs" of the album prologue. He lured her in with elaborate promises of love*

You said I'm the love of your life

Antonomasia (nickname as a proper name) that seems to allude to somewhat infantile behavior

The song is rich in images that follow in quick succession like a series of tableaux, as if the speaker is uncontrollably recalling flashes of the relationship—this fits with the idea that she cannot un-recall them, and the penultimate line that she will still see it until she dies.

You shit-talked me under the table
Talking rings and talking cradles
I wish I could un-recall
How we almost had it all
Dancing phantoms on the terrace
Are they second-hand embarrassed
That I can't get out of bed?
'Cause something counterfeit's dead
It was legendary
It was momentary
It was unnecessary
Should've let it stay buried
Oh, what a valiant roar
What a bland goodbye
The coward claimed he was a lion
I'm combing through the braids of lies
"I'll never leave" ...
"Never mind"

The three-time repetition of "talk" emphasizes that that's all it was—empty words

Swift has coined her own word here to express her deep desire to forget

Swiftian trope—combining colloquial, slang language with more poetic vocabulary to lend authenticity

Encapsulates two main themes: fakery, and death/resurrection. The "dead" is final, compared to the "never quite buried"

Tricolon adds emphasis

Yet earlier the speaker says it was "never quite buried"

This exclamation adds to the spontaneous, intimate feeling of the song

The contrast here stresses the disappointment of the eventual affair

A metaphor that echoes "tendrils tucked into a woven braid" in "But Daddy I Love Him." It's a beautiful, intimate image to express the slow unpacking of a relationship after its end (a postmortem, of sorts). It also suggests how tightly woven these lies were

Bathos—the grand, definite statement is quickly negated

Our field of dreams, engulfed in fire

Alliteration displays the tragic contrast. The "rekindled flames" ended in a destructive blaze

Your arson's match your somber eyes

There's something rather sinister and funereal about this description, as if the object of the poem set fire "in cold blood"

And I'll still see it until I die

You're the loss of my life

Succinctly places the entire blame on the object of the poem for destroying everything, as in "My Boy Only Breaks His Favorite Toys." See also the reference to "self-sabotage mode" in "The Tortured Poets Department"

As in many of Swift's songs, there's an element of prolepsis—looking into the future—as she imagines how the affair will be remembered for all time, not only by her lover but by others (as "legendary"). The significance of the cryptic title, "loml," only becomes clear in the final line of the poem, which delivers a gut-punching element of surprise—the subject is not just the "love" of her life as we have come to assume, but also the "loss" of her life. This twist of a popular idiom mirrors the idea of the "volta," or turn. It is a poetic technique that dates back at least to the Renaissance sonnet.

Unusual meter with frequent use of spondees, making every syllable "heavy." Akin to methodically going over every detail of a criminal investigation

The Smallest Man Who Ever Lived

Was any of it true? *Rhetorical*

Gazing at me starry-eyed *Known for being charming and persuasive, like the man in this song*

In your Jehovah's Witness suit

Who the fuck was that guy?

Implies he was putting on an act

You tried to buy some pills

From a friend of friends of mine

They just ghosted you

Now you know what it feels like

And I don't even want you back, I just want to know

Contrast to emphasize the effect of their affair

If rusting my sparkling summer was the goal

And I don't miss what we had, but could someone give

A message to the smallest man who ever lived? *Multiple meanings: cowardice, insignificance, or a veiled reference to his physical attributes*

Another rhethorical question

You hung me on your wall *He put the speaker on a metaphorical pedestal*

Stabbed me with your push pins

Extends the metaphor

In public, showed me off *Reminiscent of how collectors display colorful insects such as butterflies. The speaker was merely another pretty thing to add to his collection—and he was prepared to "kill" her to do so*

Then sank in stoned oblivion

'Cause once your queen had come

A loser

You treat her like an also-ran

You didn't measure up *On drugs, but also "sank like a stone"—the drugs send him down into metaphorical depths*

In any measure of a man

Could be literal or metaphorical

And I don't even want you back, I just want to know

If rusting my sparkling summer was the goal

And I don't miss what we had, but could someone give

A message to the smallest man who ever lived?

Were you sent by someone who wanted me dead?

Did you sleep with a gun underneath our bed?

Were you writing a book? Were you a sleeper cell spy?

In fifty years, will all this be declassified?

And you'll confess why you did it

And I'll say, "Good riddance"

'Cause it wasn't sexy once it wasn't forbidden

I would've died for your sins

Instead, I just died inside

And you deserve prison, but you won't get time

You'll slide into inboxes and slip through the bars

You crashed my party and your rental car

You said normal girls were boring

But you were gone by the morning

You kicked out the stage lights

But you're still performing

And in plain sight you hid

But you are what you did

And I'll forget you, but I'll never forgive

The smallest man who ever lived

Escalates into a violent crescendo with equally violent imagery

Pun (sleeper)

Language of espionage tells us his treachery feels like an actual crime

Rhetorical questions—the speaker is still trying to process

Slant rhyme: coherence is breaking down

Literal dying (framed as self-sacrifice) becomes metaphorical dying

One virtual idea (inboxes) and one literal (prison bars), but could also be metaphorical (he will never have to face the consequences of his actions)

Zeugma (crashed)

Anastrophe to illustrate his strategy of concealing his true self while out in the open

Something of a paradox—can you forget if you don't forgive? Plays on the idiom "forgive and forget"

THE SMALLEST MAN WHO EVER LIVED

[analysis]

"The Smallest Man Who Ever Lived" reads like a one-sided interrogation, which is rather fitting, given that it is pervaded by the language of espionage, criminality, and deceit. The use of second-person address ("you") creates a feeling of intimacy, as if the speaker is directly interrogating the object of the song. There are repeated rhetorical questions, as the speaker tries to understand the actions of a man—initially charming and persuasive in his "Jehovah's Witness suit"—who used and then ghosted her. The "smallest man" can be read both metaphorically—referring to his cowardice and selfishness, and inability to live up to her expectations—or potentially literally (some fans perceive it as a derogative comment on his anatomy). The song uses the language of criminality to suggest that his actions and their effects are tantamount to an actual legal crime (*Rolling Stone* journalist Brittany Spanos tweeted on the day of the song's release: "saying a man needs jail time for ghosting...she's right").

The song's frequent "and...but" structure suggests both a spontaneous, emotional stream of consciousness—very characteristic of *The Tortured Poets Department* as a whole—but also reflects the contradictory nature of the man in the song. He frustrated her expectations, made empty promises, and disappointed her with his behavior. This is also emphasized through contrasts: rusting versus sparkling, queen versus also-ran. There's quite a lot of violence in the song—stabbing, guns, crashing, kicking—which alludes to the emotional violence caused by the "smallest man." It's an uncomfortable reminder of the ways in which one might perform romance and intimacy, only to withdraw it suddenly. The song also juxtaposes two different ideas of death: the cold-blooded, violent way in which the speaker assumes the smallest man wanted her dead (with a gun underneath their bed), and the selfless, sacrificial death the speaker would have endured out of love for him. This mismatch illustrates the gulf between them, their different motives in the relationship, and the inevitable tragic outcome.

The Black Dog

"Feminine rhymes"—the speaker pauses after singing "recent," so that the song rhymes on "recent" and "secrets" even though they are not at the end. Less definite and rhythmic than traditional rhymes

I am someone who until recent events
Enjambment
You shared your secrets with
And your location, you forgot to turn it off
And so I **w**atch as you **w**alk
Into some **b**ar called The **B**lack Dog
Alliteration and slant rhyme—there's cohesion but also uncertainty
And pierce new holes in my heart
Echoes "loml"—"new" implies this grief is ongoing
You forgot to turn it off
Ambiguous—location or her heart?
And it hits me

I just don't understand
How you don't miss me in The Black Dog
When someone plays The Starting Line
Allusion to the band. Also referenced in "Fresh Out The Slammer," linking the two songs together
Internal slant rhymes
And you jump up, but she's too young to know this song
That was intertwined in the magic fabric of our dreaming
This metaphor makes nice use of a contrast between the physical and tangible (thread, fabric) and the intangible and ephemeral (dreams)
Old habits die screaming
A very Swiftian trope: taking a common phrase or idiom ("old habits die hard") and twisting it, in this case to make it more emphatic and alarming
I move through the world with the heartbroken
My longings stay unspoken
Conditional tense
Feminine rhyme that is, at some point, internal slant rhyme too (spoken/open)
And I may never open up the way I did for you
And all of those best laid plans
A common idiom, but originally from Robert Burns's poem "To a Mouse"
You said I needed a brave man
Then proceeded to play him
Until I believed it too
Combination of "brave" and "play" suggests the object was just acting the part. The rhyme is also a slant rhyme, which adds to this sense of incompleteness—he wasn't who he pretended to be
And it kills me
A more violent variation of "hits me" above

I just don't understand

How you don't miss me in the shower

And remember how my rain-soaked body

Was shakin', do you hate me?

Was it hazing? For a cruel fraternity

In "Call It What You Want," the speaker says she trusts her lover like a brother

I pledged and I still mean it

Extends the fraternity metaphor, but she's pledged to him

Old habits die screaming

Vocally screamed in the song itself

Six weeks of breathin' clean air

Cleanness as a metaphor for relationship recovery, as in "Clean"

I still miss the smoke

Possible allusions to "Daylight" and the personification of London (colloquially, "The Big Smoke")

Were you makin' fun of me

With some esoteric joke?

Now I wanna sell my house

And set fire to all my clothes

And hire a priest to come and exorcise my demons

In "invisible string," she implies that the object of the song chained her demons. In leaving, he has released them again

Even if I die screaming

And I hope you hear it

Contrast with "I hope it's nice where you are," sung to an ex-lover in "Last Kiss." This speaker is rather less magnanimous

And I hope it's shitty in The Black Dog

When someone plays The Starting Line

And you jump up, but she's too young to know this song

Magic, from the chorus above, has become "tragic"

That was intertwined in the tragic fabric of our dreaming

'Cause tail between your legs, you're leavin'

I still can't believe it

'Cause old habits die screaming

"Black dog" is a British idiom for depression. The object of the song himself could be the black dog. "Tail between your legs" reads as a bit belittling, but implies the object feels shame

THE BLACK DOG

[analysis]

The image of the black dog runs through this song, but as in so many of Swift's works, it changes meaning and significance throughout the lines. It appears to be a straightforward reference to a bar (there is one of the same name in London, to which Swifties began making pilgrimages following the release of the song), but might also be read as a metaphor for depression, and/or as a reference to the object of the song himself, since he's later referenced with his tail between his legs. Other songs on *The Tortured Poets Department* allude to the end of a relationship because of the "blues" of the man in question (most notably, "So Long, London" and "Fresh Out The Slammer"), and this song seems to fit that interpretation.

The unusual, frequent use of feminine rhyme, slant rhyme and caesura in this song give it the feeling of an unrehearsed, spontaneous monologue, which lends a sense of intimacy. Added to that, the rhetorical questions and linguistic uncertainty (anacoluthon) suggest a speaker processing her feelings and struggling to come to terms with the change in her situation now that her lover has left. The song climaxes at the end of each chorus on "screaming" (echoed in the music), but then returns to softer, more contemplative language, as if the speaker is cycling through bouts of intense grief and anger followed by more muted sadness. There are possible references to several of Swift's other songs: notice, particularly, the contrast between her hope that "it's nice where you are" in "Last Kiss" with the vindictive "I hope it's shitty in The Black Dog." This sentiment fits with Swift's description of *The Tortured Poets Department* as "Female Rage: The Musical."

Chloe or Sam or Sophia or Marcus

An image so clear to her it's almost physically present

Your hologram stumbled into my apartment

A scene of drunkenness or passion or both

Hands in the hair of somebody in darkness

Ambiguous—a faceless new lover or a room shrouded in darkness

Named Chloe or Sam or Sophia or Marcus

And I just watched it happen

There is an intriguing fan theory that the speaker is watching her lover cheat through her Ring camera

As the decade would play us for fools

Personification echoes "Peter," and the "goddess of timing" who seems to have lied

And you saw my bones out with somebody new

Similar logic to wearing one's heart on one's sleeve: she is transparent, her soul bared for all to see

Who seemed like he would've bullied you in school

And you just watched it happen

Shift from "I" to "you": both (ex)-lovers are apathetic. This song raises the heart-breaking possibility of a lost love no longer caring at all

If you want to break my cold, cold heart

Hints at irony—as if the object accused the speaker of being cold-hearted—but she insists it isn't true

Just say, "I loved you the way that you were"

If you want to tear my world apart

Suggests the speaker tried to change herself to be worthy of the object's love. It would shatter her to learn she was, in fact, good enough

Just say you've always wondered

A clever metaphor implying the saturation of the speaker's very being

You said some things that I can't unabsorb

You turned me into an idea of sorts

The object of the song loved the idea of the speaker more than the reality

You needed me but you needed drugs more

And I couldn't watch it happen

Subtle shift: rather than being passive, this time, the speaker attempts to intervene

I changed into goddesses, villains and fools

Changed plans and lovers and outfits and rules

Tricolon could be read autobiographically as Swift's industry transformations, the speaker "trying on" new identities, or the object's perspective of the speaker depending on his mood

All to outrun my desertion of you

A metaphor that suggests futility: one cannot typically outrun something (like destiny)

Formal, implying the speaker thinks of it as gravely serious or even criminal

And you just watched it

"happen" is missing—the object is even more passive than before

If you want to break my cold, cold heart

Just say, "I loved you the way that you were"

If you want to tear my world apart

Just say you've always wondered

The alternate ending is represented in the next verse by the "phantoms"

If the glint in my eye traced the depths of your sigh *Using his "sighs" (of disapproval, longing, or pain, it's unclear) as an anchor point through time travel, to then make things right from the beginning*

Mischief, intentionality

Down that passage in time

Back to the moment I crashed into you

Like so many wrecks do *Evokes "Maroon," but also their extreme passion and possible destruction*

Too impaired by my youth

Youth as a hindrance is a quietly tragic idea

To know what to do

Neatness and reciprocity in the rhyme scheme of this verse align with the theme of going back and making everything right

So if I sell my apartment

And you have some kids with an internet starlet

Will that **m**ake your **m**emory **f**ade **f**rom this scarlet **m**aroon *Allusion to "Maroon" and possibly "Red." A desperate desire to rid herself of "burning red" flashbacks that follow lost love*

Like it never happened

Conditional to express regret

Could it be enough to just float in your orbit *Weighing up the possibility of still loving her ex-lover from afar, passively, without pain. The power dynamic is uneven*

Can we **w**atch our phantoms like **w**atching **w**ild horses *A love song by the Rolling Stones. Also suggests something capricious, untamed, and out of reach*

Polyptoton of "watch" amplifies the speaker's desire to be passive

The doppelgängers of the speaker and object in an alternate universe where things went differently

Cooler in theory but not if you force it *Passive observation does not fit the reality of her emotional involvement. Or a pun: wishing for cooler relations rather than the residually fiery ones now*

To be, it just didn't happen

So if you want to break my cold, cold heart

A plea

Say you loved me

And if you want to tear my world apart

Say you'll always wonder

Shift to future tense reflects the way this song operates in the future and conditional: anxiety about what is to come, and speculation about what might have been

Cause I wonder

Will I always

Will I always wonder?

Meta: wondering about wondering. Fits the idea of forever wondering about the "one that got away"

CHLOE OR SAM OR SOPHIA OR MARCUS

[analysis]

Often nicknamed "Chloe et al." (or COSOSOM), this song is a fan favorite from the second half of *The Tortured Poets Department,* perhaps owing to its recognizable sentiment. It muses on the way we self-destructively obsess over our ex-lover's new romances in the wake of a relationship ending; the song's title seems to refer to the vagueness of this new imagined lover; specificity is not important, it's painful either way. It also hints at a story involving the object of the song's addiction, and the speaker's inability to watch it unfold, as well as a speaker who is constantly changing herself but whose greatest fear is that, actually, she was loved just as she was—perhaps, if we read it autobiographically, Swift's reflection on the way fame can negatively impact romantic love. The grieving speaker considers the possibility of being able to love the object of the song from afar, and one day simply idly speculate on what their alternate selves—"phantoms"—might have done, but gradually accepts the impossibility of this forced outcome.

Like "So Long, London" and "The Black Dog," COSOSOM plays around with rhyme and caesura to mimic a stream of consciousness, coming across as raw and confessional. It also uses caesura to suggest the speaker pausing to collect herself on certain words, overcome with emotion. In this way, it's characteristic of *The Tortured Poets Department,* perhaps Swift's most "unfiltered"-sounding album. There's very little perfect rhyme, lending the song a more conversational feel that lacks neatness and coherence, aptly for a song that deals with wondering about wondering, and the messy end of a love affair. The song culminates in uncertainty, reflecting another relatable sentiment: our tendency to ponder "what might have been" in life.

How Did It End?

Archaic, as if read in a courtroom

We hereby conduct this postmortem

An investigation into the cause of death (in this case, of a relationship)

He was a hot house flower to my outdoorsman

A rich metaphor that evokes The Signature of All Things, Elizabeth Gilbert. It may imply that the pair were mismatched, the object was so rare and precious he had to be sheltered, or that he lacked the kind of authenticity pursued by the speaker

Our maladies were such we could not cure them

Relationship as an actual affliction. This would explain the need for a postmortem

And so a touch that was my birthright became foreign

Recalls "exile;" a love that once seemed fundamentally right has become strange

Come one, come all

Evokes the circus: this postmortem will be entertainment to certain audiences, as in "I Can Do It With A Broken Heart"

It's happenin' again

Dialogismus

The empathetic hunger descends

Sarcastic: people will pretend to care in order to glean as much gossip as possible

We'll tell no one

"We" shifts and merges in meaning

Except all of our friends

We must know

How did it end?

(Uh-oh)

(Uh-oh-oh-oh)

Paradox to represent fakery of those who lend a sympathetic ear to obtain gossip

We were blind to unforeseen circumstances

Implies that they were doubly blind, and hints at a naivety—or worse, willful ignorance

We learned the right steps to different dances (ohh)

Recalls the reference to waltzing in "loml." They were fundamentally on different trajectories

And fell victim to interlopers' glances

Adultery or relentless speculation. "Victim" hints at culpability and crime: were the "interlopers" the true assailants?

Lost the game of chance, what are the chances?

Soon they'll go home to their husbands

Smug 'cause they know they can trust him

Ironic

Then feverishly calling their cousins (ohh)

Same semantic field as "maladies," suggesting an unhealthy obsession

Guess who we ran into at the shops?

Walking in circles like she was lost

Evokes "cardigan": "chasing shadows in the grocery line," and reiterates how the speaker is cycling the thoughts in her head

Didn't you hear?

They called it all off

One gasp and then

A reaction from gossip, or a dying breath as in the coming "death rattle"

How did it end?

Say it once again with feeling

Sarcastic, as if the speaker is being asked to perform for a hungry crowd's entertainment

How the death rattle breathing

Silenced as the soul was leaving

The deflation of our dreaming

The references to "gasp," "death rattle" and "deflation" contribute to the personification of the relationship as a human body, whose lungs have emptied for the last time. This recalls the lack of a pulse in "You're Losing Me" and stopping CPR in "So Long, London"

Leaving me bereft and reeling

My beloved ghost and me

A reel is also a dance, fitting with the reference to learning dance steps above

Sitting in a tree

D-Y-I-N-G

Another slightly archaic word, which adds to the grandiose tone of the song

It's happenin' again

How did it end?

Recalls the children's chant "sitting in a tree, K-I-S-S-I-N-G." The tragic twist seems to suggest the childishness of gossipers, when its death is so heavily felt by the speaker. It may also indicate the speaker's own feelings of naivety

I can't pretend like I understand

How did it end?

Unanswered, rhetorical

Come one, come all

It's happening again

The empathetic hunger descends

We'll tell no one

Except all of our friends

But I still don't know

How did it end?

The song plays out, steadily, like the "reeling" mind of someone still trying to understand

HOW DID IT END?

[analysis]

"How Did It End?" raises the somewhat philosophical question of when a relationship is truly over: the opening references to a postmortem suggest the speaker is searching for the ultimate "cause of death," and reflecting on the death throes of the affair. This fits with a tradition in Swift's work of depicting relationships as living bodies, with breath and a beating heart: here, the sick body ("maladies") could not be cured and ultimately let out its dying breath. However, the song is also a powerful reflection on the "empathetic hunger" that attends the end of celebrity relationships. As fan account @tweetsrichochet pointed out, Swift's autobiographical songwriting has bred public entitlement: "with every new heartbreak, many of her fans and detractors alike have come to feel that they *deserve* to know 'how it ended.'" The speaker offers tantalizing hints as to the cause of the breakup (different personalities, as suggested by the hothouse flower comparison; and different goals, as suggested by the dances reference), but ultimately suggests that the hungry audience will never be satisfied, especially since the speaker doesn't know the cause herself; the song ending on a rhetorical question is proof of this.

"How Did It End?" plays with different meanings of the word "we," referring both to the speaker and her lover but also to proponents of celebrity gossip and/or Swift's fans. It juxtaposes the language of entertainment (musicals and the circus) with the language of tragedy, to explore the ways in which celebrity heartbreak serves as a form of diverting enjoyment to many. The result is somewhat uncomfortable, reminding the listener of his or her role in this postmortem hunger and the inappropriateness of gleefully spectating and analyzing slow death. There's a hint of sarcasm and bitterness here that we also find in "But Daddy I Love Him" and "Who's Afraid of Little Old Me?"

The Prophecy

Hand on the throttle

Thought I caught lightning in a bottle

Oh, but it's gone again

And it was written

I got cursed like Eve got bitten

Oh, was it punishment?

Pad around when I get home

I guess a lesser woman would've lost hope

A greater woman wouldn't beg

But I looked to the sky and said

Please

I've been on my knees

Change the prophecy

Don't want money

Just someone who wants my company

Let it once be me

Who do I have to speak to

About if they can redo

The prophecy?

Cards on the table

Mine play out like fools in a fable, oh

It was sinking in

Slow is the quicksand

Poison blood from the wound of the pricked hand

Rhyming couplet and internal rhyme echo the speaker's feeling of satisfaction that she has indeed "caught lightning in a bottle," but this is a complex metaphor. It suggests taking something potentially negative and making it work for her, using its power; it also suggests trapping potent energy, which is where its idiomatic meaning comes from: achieving great success

"It was written" summons Biblical texts and ancient prophecies

Indicates control

"Oh" and "again" suggest quiet, if expected, disappointment

Passive voice

Technically, Eve bit the forbidden fruit. This might be a deliberate mistake to say the speaker has only herself to blame for her "curse"

Implies the comfort of home, but also aligns with forthcoming wolf imagery

Internal rhyme

If we follow the Eve analogy; yes. This raises the question of what for and by whom?

We have to wait for the plea in the chorus here, creating suspense

An image of humility, prayer, and prostrate desperation

Huge amount of assonance creates a prayer-like quality. The "ee" sound is also evocative of screaming, which fits with the desperate nature of the speaker's plea

Poignantly naive line, since the whole point of prophecies is that they are set in stone

Tarot cards predicting the future: the combined metaphor (with poker) suggests her fate is clear for all to see

Conjures Sleeping Beauty. Implies that her emotions are toxic to those around her or that she is irreparably harmed

Oh, still I dream of him

Ambiguous: the one who poisoned her or the true love

chorus repeats

And I sound like an infant

Self-loathing

Feeling like the very last drops of an ink pen

Implies exhaustion and waning creativity (somewhat ironically, for a song that is in fact very creative)

A greater woman stays cool

Pun

But I howl like a wolf at the moon

Pain and isolation. Wolves howl at the moon as a way of communicating with the rest of their pack

And I look unstable

Gathered with a coven round a sorceress table

Reminiscent of "willow." Redolent of fairy tale, female solidarity, and connects with the witch-hunting imagery of "mad woman." The speaker is embracing or poking fun at a symbol of the patriarchy's worst fears

A greater woman has faith

But even statues crumble if they're made to wait

I'm so afraid I sealed my fate

No **s**ign of **s**oulmates

I'm just a paperweight

In shades of greige

A metaphor that pairs with the "ink pen" earlier; the speaker feels like a burden, but a tedious, uninteresting one too. Paperweights are often attractive but functional—not truly special, merely useful

apathy here

Spending my last coin so someone will tell me

It'll be ok

"My last coin" is a somewhat poetic way of expressing money, again evoking a fairytale aesthetic, but suggests a limit to what it can and cannot buy

chorus repeats

Hand on the throttle

Thought I caught lightning in a bottle, oh

But it's gone again

Pad around when I get home

I guess a lesser woman would've lost hope

A greater woman wouldn't beg

But I looked to the sky and said

Please

Ending with a vulnerable plea finishes the song on a poignant note, which also leaves the listener in suspense, not knowing whether the request was granted

THE PROPHECY

[analysis]

Drawing on imagery from mythology and fairy tale, Swift here explores the idea of one's fate and destiny seeming "sealed" and unchangeable. The song reads as semi-autobiographical, exploring the pressures of fame and success, particularly as they impact one's romantic life and desire to find authentic love and a soulmate. Swift uses several images and metaphors from elsewhere in her discography, but shifts them subtly in ways that poignantly emphasize a feeling of exhaustion, uselessness, anxiety, and frustration. "The Prophecy" might be read as a sister song to "Cassandra," which immediately follows it on *The Tortured Poets Department*. Cassandra is a figure from Greek mythology, a Trojan princess cursed always to utter true prophecies but have no one believe her. "The Prophecy" seems to explore the other side of the coin: a woman who refuses to believe the truth of the prophecies uttered to her. Both songs invoke women from ancient literature and legend (Cassandra and Eve) to explore female frustration, the social burdens and expectations placed on women, and the idea of a fundamental, objective truth that we might long to manipulate, but cannot. The voice is often tragically naive, implying a childish desire to simply find the person in charge and ask them to change the future.

In addition to its rich imagery—which corresponds perhaps most closely with that in Swift's song "willow"—"The Prophecy" plays with assonance and rhyme in ways that create a tight correspondence between lines and words, reflecting the "fixedness" of one's fate being sealed and inexorable. There is a slow, lumbering quality between the double rhyme of "quicksand" and "pricked hand," mirroring the physicality of the quicksand as much as the "sinking" realization that the speaker cannot escape her fate. We also find subtle allusions to a long literary history of women "frozen" or fixed in time, including Charles Dickens's Miss Havisham of *Great Expectations*, whose ghost also haunts Swift's "right where you left me" off of *evermore*.

CONCLUSION

These words are ours.

The story isn't just Taylor Swift's anymore. These are the stories of all of us, and we find them in every twist and turn of Swift's lyricism. My sweeping, sloping annotations can only take us so far: these lyrics can't stop, won't stop moving. They perpetually take on new significance in our lives and our imaginations. Like a mirrorball, we see a million versions of ourselves in these songs, which is perhaps why they have resonated so strongly with so many of us over the years. Call it what you want: poetry truly comes to life with the reader, or listener, and the ultimate meaning is yours to keep, forever and always. As you reread the manuscript, I hope you'll feel inspired by this brief trip to Taylor's shore, and continue to draw invisible strings between words, forms, and meaning for evermore.

How did it end? With you, Dear Reader.

glossary of literary terms

Adnomination – the repetition of root words, though the rest of the word may change. For example, "got **love**struck, went straight to my head, got **love**sick all over my bed."

Alliteration – the repetition of the same letter or sound at the beginning of several words. For example, "I **p**olish **p**lates until they **gl**eam and **gl**isten."

Allusion – a reference to another work, like a song, novel, piece of art, band, etc. For example, "when someone plays **The Starting Line.**"

Anacoluthon – when a speaker breaks the grammatical flow of the sentence they are uttering, either to change course or interrupt themselves. For example, "I hope she'll be a beautiful fool, who takes my spot next to you, no I didn't mean that" or "and all of those best laid plans, you said I needed a brave man."

Analepsis – a flashback, e.g., "I do recall the smell of the rain"; "and there we are again in the middle of the night."

Anaphora – repetition of the same word or phrase at the beginning of successive phrases. For example, "**karma is** my boyfriend, **karma is** a god, **karma is** the breeze in my hair on the weekend."

Anastrophe – inverting the traditional, grammatical word order of a sentence to emphasis a particular word or idea. For example, "**long** were the nights"; "**green** was the grass."

Antanaclasis – the use of a word twice in two different senses in the same sentence or phrase. For example, "you **keep** his shirt, he **keeps** his word": the first "keep" is literal, the second, metaphorical. This is closely related to **zeugma**.

Anthypophora – asking a question and then immediately answering it yourself. For example, "the idea you had of me, who was she? A never-needy, ever-lovely jewel."

Antimetabole – the repetition of a sentence, but this time in reverse order. For example, "I don't trust nobody and nobody trusts me."

Antonomasia – a phrase or nickname taking the place of a proper name. For example, "Miss Americana," "Mr Perfectly Fine."

Apostrophe – direct address to someone or something who cannot respond, usually via an exclamation. For example, "oh back up, baby back up, did you forget everything?"

Assonance – repetition of words with shared vowel sounds, creating a feeling of rhyme. For example, the "ee" sound in "who wants my compan**y**, let it once b**e** m**e**, who do I have to sp**ea**k to?"

Asyndeton – a list of words without conjunctions (e.g., "and," "or") in between. For example, "my heart, my hips, my body, my love." The opposite is **polysyndeton.**

Bathos (or **bathetic**) – anticlimax, often involving an abrupt shift in mood from the poetic to the mundane, or the sublime to the ridiculous. For example, "I find the artifacts, cried over a hat."

Caesura – a pause, often indicated by a comma or full stop. For example, "thinkin', how much sad did you, think I had, did you, think I had in me?"

Chiasmus – the second half of a sentence or phrase mirrors the first in terms of parts of speech (but without being an exact repetition–that is **antimetabole**). For example, "luck of the draw only draws the unlucky."

Compound adjective – placing two words together with a hyphen in the middle to create a new, expressive adjective. For example, "a **never-needy**, **ever-lovely** jewel."

Conditional tense – used to describe what might happen, hypothetically, in the future, or what *might have* happened in the past. For example, "if you **would've** blinked then I **would've** looked away at the first glance"; "I **could** show you incredible things."

Consonance – repetition of words with shared consonants, creating a feeling of rhyme. For example, "**b**alanci**ng** on **b**reak**ing.**"

Dactyl – a poetic foot consisting of three syllables, with the first stressed and the second and third unstressed. For example, the "boulevard" in "sunrise **boul**evard"; "**swim**ming pool."

Dialogismus – temporarily speaking as someone else. For example, "Who's Taylor Swift anyway?"

Ekphrasis – describing in detail a work of art or image so it feels like you're telling a story within a story. For example, "there is a video I found, from back when I was three, you set up a paint set in the kitchen, and you're talking to me."

Enjambment – when you must immediately read from one end of a line of poetry to the beginning of the next, to complete the sentence or idea. For example, "you're so much older and wiser and I [new line] wait by the door like I'm just a kid."

Epistrophe – the opposite of **anaphora;** repetition of a word at the *end* of a series of phrases. For example, "I'm the only one of **me**, baby that's the fun of **me.**"

Epizeuxis – the repetition of a word for emphasis, often in the same sentence. For example, "I've never been a natural, all I do is **try, try, try**."

Feminine rhyme – a rhyme between the stressed syllables of two or more words. For example, "water" and "daughter." This might also be slant rhyme. For example, "**re**cent" and "**se**crets"; "**prom**ise" and "**hon**est"; "**less**on" and "**stress**ing."

Homophone – words that sound the same but mean different things. For example, "mourning" and "morning."

Hyperbole – exaggeration. For example, "catastrophic blues," "insurmountable grief."

Idiom – a common phrase or saying, often with a metaphorical meaning. For example, "all's well that end's well," "out of the woods."

In media res – beginning a narrative in the middle of things (without setting up background and context). For example, "Drew looks at me," "was any of it true?"

Internal rhyme – when the rhyme doesn't fall at the end of two lines of poetry, as is traditional, but instead is between two words or phrases within the line itself. For example, "all I felt was **shame**, and you held my lifeless **frame**." Internal rhyme can also be **slant rhyme**, for example, "you are an expert at **sorry**, and keeping lines **blurry.**"

Juxtaposition – the placement of two contrasting words or concepts side by side. For example, "**rusting** my **sparkling** summer."

Linked rhyme – when the word at the end of a line rhymes with the first word of the next. For example, "Oh, a simple **complication, miscommunications** lead to fallout."

Metaphor – comparing two things by saying one thing *is* something else – it's a stronger comparison than a **simile.** For example, "the way you move is like a full-on rainstorm, and I'm a house of cards": the first part is a simile, the second a metaphor. Or "we were a fresh page on the desk." An **extended metaphor** is when the metaphor recurs and develops throughout the song or poem.

Metonymy – referring to something or someone using something associated with it. For example, "So long, **London**"; "your **Brooklyn** broke my skin and bones."

Objective correlative – where emotions are implied or associated with an object. For example, "please picture me in the **weeds**, before I learned civility, I used to scream ferociously."

Onomatopoeia – a word that sounds like the sound it describes, e.g., "**clink, clink**."

Oxymoron – a form of **juxtaposition** in which the words or ideas placed side-by-side contradict one another or cancel one another out. For example, "I've never heard

silence quite this **loud**."

Paradox – two contrasting things together that seem impossible but could make sense, for example "standing alone in a crowded room."

Parallelism – when sentences or clauses seem to echo or reflect each other, in structure and/or ideas. For example, "you do what you want 'cause I'm not what you wanted."

Passive voice – when something is done *to* someone, rather than someone *doing* something. For example, "I got cursed," "to be messed with."

Pathetic fallacy – where the weather or setting is described in such a way that it seems to reflect the mood of the speaker or theme of the song/poem. For example, "what a rainy ending given to a perfect day."

Plosive sounds – "p," "t," "k," "g," "d," and "b" sounds – like making a small "explosion" with your mouth. (e.g., "**b**lood and **b**ruise").

Polyptoton – the repetition of words derived from the same root. For example, "you had a **speech**, you're **speech**less" or "you had to **kill** me, but it **kill**ed you just the same."

Polysyndeton – a list of things with conjunctions (e.g., "and," "or") in between. For example, "all you are is mean, **and** a liar, **and** pathetic, **and** alone in life, **and** mean."

Present participles – verbs ending in "ing" to illustrate ongoing action. For example, "ask**ing** God if he could play it again."

Prolepsis – the opposite of a flashback; a flash-forward, e.g., "let's fast forward to three hundred take-out coffees later."

Prosopopoeia – a form of personification, where an inanimate object is discussed, or acts, as if they were a person. For example, "I ask the traffic lights if it will be alright, they say 'I don't know'." The opposite is **antiprosopopoeia:** comparing a person to an inanimate object.

Reported speech – narrating what someone else has said, using speech marks. For example, "he says, 'look up'."

Rhetorical question – asking a question to which one does not expect to receive a reply, since the answer is self-evident and/or the speaker wants to make a point. For example, "don't you think I was too young to be messed with?"

Second person address – "you" in a song, speech, or text. For example, "you keep his shirt."

Semantic field – an area of meaning, to which several words relate. For example, "did you sleep with a **gun** underneath our bed, were you writing a book, were you a **sleeper cell spy**, in fifty years will all this be **declassified**, and you'll **confess** why you did it" – these are all words in the semantic field of crime/espionage.

Sibilance – repetition of "s" sounds. For example, "left my **s**carf there at your **s**i**s**ter'**s** house."

Simile – comparing two things by saying one thing is *like* or *as* something else. For example, "with your words **like** knives," "rare **as** the glimmer of a comet in the sky."

Slant rhyme – a rhyme that is not complete or perfect, often relying on assonance or consonance. Also known as **half rhyme**. For example, "unspoken" and "open"; "street" and "suddenly"; "again" and "friend."

Spondee – a poetic foot consisting of two stressed syllables. For example, "one look, dark room, meant just for you" consists of four spondees.

Superlative – best or worst/most + adjective/adjective + "est." For example, "the pretti**est** lady," "the **worst** thing that I ever did." Closely linked to **hyperbole**.

Synecdoche – when a part of something is used to refer to the whole. For example, "your sweet disposition and my wide-eyed gaze," to signify the two people involved.

Tricolon – three phrases or images in a row. For example, "screaming, crying, perfect storms."

Trochee – a poetic foot consisting of a stressed syllable followed by an unstressed syllable. For example, "**room**mate's **cheap**-ass **screw**-top **ro**sé" is a series of trochees, with the stress on the part in bold.

Zeugma – applying one word to two others, but in different senses, usually literal and metaphorical. For example, "you **crashed** my **party** and your rental **car**," "you **held** your **breath** and the **door**." **Mesozeugma** is when the one word occurs in the middle of the line, such as "the moon was high like your friends were."

index

Note: Page numbers in *italics* indicate the location of the song's lyrics and analysis.

about the author

Elly McCausland, Ph.D. is an award-winning author and professor of English Literature at Ghent University, Belgium. A devoted Swiftie, Dr. McCausland launched the Masters course, "English Literature (Taylor's Version)" to international attention. She has been featured on CNN, BBC Global News, Emily Ratajkowski's podcast *EmRata*, and in *The Guardian*, *USA Today*, and other major media outlets. She is a specialist in children's literature, a keen traveler, a food writer, and a tea and houseplant enthusiast. You can follow Dr. McCausland @swifterature1989 on social media and at her website Swifterature.com.